A GUIDE FOR T

WHAT DO YOU REALLY WANT?

HOW TO SET A GOAL AND GO FOR IT!

Beverly K. Bachel

free spirit
PUBLISHING®

Library of Congress Cataloging-in-Publication Data
Names: Bachel, Beverly K., 1957–
Title: What do you really want? : how to set a goal and go for it! a guide for teens / Beverly K. Bachel.
Description: Revised & Updated Edition. | Golden Valley : Free Spirit Publishing, 2016. | Revised edition of the author's What do you really want?, 2001. | Description based on print version record and CIP data provided by publisher; resource not viewed.
Identifiers: LCCN 2015050599 (print) | LCCN 2015039910 (ebook) | ISBN 9781631980992 (Web pdf) | ISBN 9781631981005 (epub) | ISBN 9781631980305 (paperback) | ISBN 1631980300
Subjects: LCSH: Goal (Psychology) | Success—Psychological aspects. | BISAC: JUVENILE NONFICTION / Social Issues / Self-Esteem & Self-Reliance. | JUVENILE NONFICTION / School & Education. | JUVENILE NONFICTION / Social Issues / Values & Virtues.
Classification: LCC BF505.G6 (print) | LCC BF505.G6 B33 2016 (ebook) | DDC 153.8—dc23
LC record available at http://lccn.loc.gov/2015050599

Reading Level Grades 7 & Up; Interest Level Ages 11 & Up;
Fountas & Pinnell Guided Reading Level Z

Edited by Jana Branch, Darsi Dreyer, Elizabeth Verdick, and Alison Behnke
Cover and interior design by Colleen Rollins

10 9 8 7 6 5 4 3 2 1
Printed in the United States of America
S18860216

Free Spirit Publishing Inc.
6325 Sandburg Road, Suite 100
Golden Valley, MN 55427-3674
(612) 338-2068
help4kids@freespirit.com
www.freespirit.com

To Steve—thanks for all your love and support.

CONTENTS

Reproducible Forms

You can download and print these forms at
www.freespirit.com/WDYRW-forms. *Use password* **2achieve**.

FOREWORD: A NOTE FROM ANN BANCROFT

"Getting through high school and college is one of my greatest achievements." —Ann Bancroft, teacher, explorer, and author

I have always loved nature and the outdoors—and I've always had a hunger for adventure. When I was eight years old, I led my own mini-expeditions, convincing my cousins to join me on backyard camping trips in the middle of winter. (We lived in Minnesota!) At twelve, I learned about Sir Ernest Shackleton's legendary 1914 Antarctic voyage on the ship the *Endurance*, which became trapped in sea ice just one day's sail from reaching Antarctica. The ship eventually sank, leaving its crew stranded for nearly two years. (Thankfully everyone survived.) From then on, I knew I wanted to be a polar explorer.

As a teen, my goal was to go to college and become a teacher. Because I had a learning disability, school wasn't easy for me. In fact, some days felt like a torment. But my goal to teach kept me focused on the future.

Today, I'm both a teacher and an explorer. I'm also the first woman to ski across the ice to both the North and South Poles. I had to overcome many obstacles along the way, but I'm living my dream and doing what I feel I was meant to do. And I know you can, too. No matter how impossible it may seem sometimes, you really do have the power to set your own course. It's not easy, but it is rewarding. And your achievements—no matter how big or small—will stay with you for life.

If I could offer you only one piece of advice, it would be this: never accept "no" when it comes to pursuing your dreams. Believe in yourself and what you want to do, so you can get what you really want out of life. The skills you'll learn from this book—including how to set goals, build a support team, and keep yourself motivated—will help you set your course and make the most of your life. And this new and revised version, which covers the entire journey from inspiration to celebration, makes it even easier to put the power of goal-setting to work for you.

Whatever your dream might be, remember that you've got what it takes to achieve it. Now, get going!

Ann Bancroft is the founder of Bancroft Arnesen Explore (yourexpedition.com), an organization that empowers young people to achieve their dreams and explore issues that affect the world. Ann is also the founder of the Ann Bancroft Foundation (annbancroftfoundation.org), a nonprofit that gives girls the chance to live their dreams and reach their full potential. A popular speaker on the topics of teamwork, leadership, and goal setting, Ann draws on her experience making land, sea, and ice expeditions all around the world. She visits schools often and offers several kids' education programs, including "Dare to Dream," which was developed in conjunction with the author of this book.

INTRODUCTION

"Never underestimate the power of dreams and the influence of the human spirit. We are all the same in this notion: The potential for greatness lives within each of us." —Wilma Rudolph, Olympic track-and-field athlete

What are some of your dreams? Your hopes? We all have them. And it's fun to imagine the amazing things you might do, be, achieve, learn, or have someday. But what about today? Are you doing anything right now to make your hopes and dreams come true? When you hear yourself saying, "I wish . . ." or "I dream . . ." or "I really hope . . ." or "If only I could . . ." it's time to act. This book can help. How do I know? Because I've used the information in this book to reach my own goals. From making new friends to buying my first car, from improving my golf game to starting a business, goal setting has helped me accomplish all sorts of things—including writing this book (which for me is a dream come true).

When I was your age, I had lots of hopes and dreams. I knew there were thousands of possibilities out there, but I wasn't sure how to make them real. I wish someone had shown me how to set goals. It wasn't until I was an adult that I understood that goal setting is something you can learn— and even excel at—on your own.

ABOUT THIS BOOK

This book explains the why, what, and how of goal setting, so you can set and reach goals yourself. You'll discover what goals are, why they matter, and how you can use them to get what you *really* want. Throughout the book, watch for the "Hot Tip" boxes, where you'll find tools and advice for reaching your goals, and for "Goal Getters in Action," where you'll read stories from dozens of teens I interviewed. They're people just like you who've used goal setting to improve their lives. They live in small towns and big cities across North America and beyond. Their aspirations, personalities, and outlooks on life are as unique as their schools, families, friendships, and communities. No two are alike, but they do share a strong commitment to improving their lives and their world.

In addition to these all-new stories, this revised edition of *What Do You Really Want?* reflects new research on goal setting and includes expanded information and an updated list of resources. All of this will give you the practical skills you need to get what you really want—today, tomorrow, and for the rest of your life.

You'll also find forms that you can download, print, and then fill out on your own. (See page vi for download instructions.) Or you can photocopy or scan the forms. These forms will help you figure out your goals, plan and keep track of them, and most importantly, *go after them!* Even if you're tempted to write directly in this book, please don't (especially if it's from the library). Instead, copy, scan, or download and print the forms. This way, you can rework them if you need to—or complete them again and again for each and every goal.

The bottom line is that how you use this book is up to you. You can read it straight through, dive deep into a specific chapter, or browse the sections that seem most interesting. You can seek out inspiration by reading those "Goal Getters in Action" pieces I mentioned, and you can learn from others by using the forms called "Conversation Starters." On page 95, you'll even find out how to recruit a Goal Buddy who could read the book along with you. However you choose to read the book, you'll want to create a Goal Tracker where you can keep a record of your goals and your progress. To get started on it, turn to page 12.

And remember, this book is intended to be a guide that you return to again and again. So don't just stick it on a shelf and forget about it! Instead, put it someplace—on your night-stand, in your backpack, by your computer—where you'll see it often. That way, you'll have a constant reminder to make the most of your life by going for what you really want.

What goals will you set for yourself? What hurdles will you overcome to reach them? Who will you turn to for help? How will you inspire yourself (and others) along the way? What will you do to celebrate reaching your goals? And then, what new goals will you set? There's no way to know until you dive in and get started.

Along the way, know that I believe in you and your ability to succeed. Also know that I'm here to help! I'd like to hear your questions and learn about your goals. You can email me at **help4kids@freespirit.com**. Or, send letters to:

Beverly K. Bachel
c/o Free Spirit Publishing
6325 Sandburg Road, Suite 100
Golden Valley, MN 55427-3674

PART 1

WHY GOALS MATTER

WHAT'S A GOAL?

> "A dream is just a dream. A goal is a dream with a plan and a deadline." —Harvey Mackay, author and business owner

How did:

Twin sisters create a charitable organization that has brightened the lives of thousands of families in crisis?

A young cancer survivor raise more than $50,000 for her invention of a backpack that makes it easier for kids with cancer to get around with their medical equipment?

A student who didn't speak English when he started school in the United States go on to become school president?

They did it the same way you can: by setting goals.

But . . . what *is* a goal, exactly?

Well, a goal is something you *want*, of course! But there's more to it than that. A goal is also something you're willing to work for, whether it takes days, weeks, months, years—or even a lifetime—to achieve.

Maybe you want to develop a new habit or break an old one. Maybe you want to meet new people or get better grades. Perhaps you want to learn to play guitar, earn a spot on the team, get a summer job, go to college, or travel. Maybe you wish you were brave enough to stand up to someone who picks on you, strong enough to climb a mountain, or handy enough to build a bookcase. Maybe you wish you could cure cancer, end poverty, or clean up the world's air and water.

Hot Tip

Hopes and dreams are in your mind and in your heart—where they may stay forever unless you bring them to life. Goals help you do that. They make your hopes and dreams real by producing tangible results.

Whatever you're considering, ask yourself: *Do I only **wish** it . . . or do I want it to be **real?***

If you want it to be real, it's time to get goaling.

What if you've never had many (or any) goals? What if you've had goals but never reached them? What if you have goals now but never seem to achieve them? There's good news. You can learn to set and reach goals—even if you haven't had much experience or success in the past. Like any other skill—tying your shoes, dribbling a basketball, speaking a new language—the more you practice, the better you get.

TOP 10 LIST (REASONS GOALS ARE WORTH HAVING)

Reason #1: Goals help you be who you want to be. You can have all the dreams in the world, but if you don't act on them, how will you become who you want to be, or get where you want to go? When you know how to set a goal and go for it, you create a roadmap that takes you toward what you really want, step by step.

Reason #2: Goals stretch your comfort zone. As you pursue your goals, you may feel nervous or uncomfortable about some things, such as talking to new people, interviewing for a job, or asking adults for advice. Pushing yourself past your comfort zone is a great way to grow. It's also a safe way to take healthy risks.

Reason #3: Goals boost your confidence. When you set a goal and reach it, you prove to yourself and others that you've got what it takes to get things done. And when you do, you feel better about yourself—and better able to take on new challenges.

Reason #4: Goals give your life purpose. Goals show you—and the world—what you value. They also give you direction. When you're going after your goals, you're less likely to waste time or feel bored or restless.

"When I don't have goals, I spend more time with people who are just going with the flow. When I do have goals, I hang out with people who really want to get their lives together." —Anna, 14

Reason #5: Goals help you rely on yourself. No matter your age, you don't have to let other people decide your life. You can take charge by setting goals and making plans to reach them. In fact, once you get into the goal-setting habit, you'll notice that you feel more independent. (And people around you will notice your new independence, too!)

Reason #6: Goals encourage you to trust your decisions. You're at a point in life where you're making more decisions at home and at school. Sometimes, it's easy to go along with the crowd or be swayed by what other people want you to do. But when you keep your goals in mind, choices become clearer and decisions become easier.

Reason #7: Goals help you turn the impossible into the possible. Goal setting breaks down seemingly out-of-reach dreams into small, manageable steps, which will help you turn your "someday" dreams into real-life accomplishments.

"I work a lot harder when I have goals than when I don't."
—Alec, 15

Reason #8: Goals prove that you can make a difference. Are your goals about changing your own life? Are they about changing the lives of others? Both? Whatever you set out to do, goal setting helps you achieve it and see clear results.

Reason #9: Goals improve your outlook on life. Goals help you move forward, which is much better than sitting still or going nowhere. This momentum is a real energizer. And you'll feel more positive, guaranteed.

"Achieving goals that matter makes me happy." —Clare, 15

Reason #10: Goals create feelings of satisfaction. Studies show that people who set and reach goals perform at higher levels and are more satisfied with themselves. In fact, if you look at the goal setters you know or admire (friends, family members, teachers, business owners, community leaders, athletes, celebrities), you'll see people who are proud of their success and eager to achieve more.

Bonus reason: Goals help break negative habits. If you have a habit you'd like to break—oversleeping, gossiping, biting your nails, or playing too many video games, goal setting can help replace these behaviors with more positive ones.

3 GOAL MYTHS (DON'T BELIEVE THEM FOR A SECOND)

Myth #1: Who needs goals? I'll be fine without them. False! Success doesn't just happen by accident or sheer luck. It's more often the result of having a clear destination in mind and working hard to reach it. Doing so can be very satisfying. You might even find that having goals gives you extra energy to put forth your best effort.

Myth #2: I have to wait until a specific date to set goals. Contrary to what many people think, the start of a new year or a new school year isn't the only time (or even the best time) to set goals or begin making changes. In fact, there's no time like the present. Start right now and you'll be that much closer to reaching your goal.

Myth #3: I have to do it all by myself. It's true that setting and reaching goals is a personal process. But this doesn't mean you can't ask for help along the way. Believe it or not, there are people in your life—family, friends, teachers, coaches, and even some people you haven't met yet—who will want to help you in any way they can. Having their support can make pursuing your goals easier and more exciting!

3 GOAL TRUTHS (BELIEVE THEM FOR A LIFETIME)

Truth #1: Goals matter. Talk to any successful person—kid, teen, or adult—who has done something you admire, and chances are he or she will say it all started with a goal. Goals help you project yourself into the future, and it is this ability more than any other that determines success. Goals also help enhance your physical, mental, and emotional well-being.

Truth #2: Not enough people have goals. Studies show that only about three out of every one hundred people set goals. Even fewer actually write them down. (As you'll find out later in this book, writing down your goals is an important step toward reaching them.)

Truth #3: You can be someone who *does* have goals—a Goal Getter! Being a Goal Getter is within your reach. And it's simpler than you think. Let me show you how with a few basic steps:

- ✔ Think of something you want to do or achieve.
- ✔ Write it down on a piece of paper.
- ✔ Post the paper where you can see it.

Congratulations! You just did three things that every successful Goal Getter does. You thought of a goal, you wrote it down, and you made it visible.

GOAL GETTERS iN ACTiON

Friends On and Off the Field

Fifteen-year-old **Clare**, who lives in a Los Angeles suburb, loves playing soccer. The only thing she likes more is playing soccer with her friends, so Clare scored big when she found a community league that combined both. "For me, it's a totally different game when I'm surrounded by friends," she says.

Clare also had a goal of making her high school freshman-sophomore team. "To achieve that, I had to push myself, but I didn't want to push so hard that I stopped having fun," says Clare. Her determination paid off. She made the team, and so did some of her friends. Now Clare has a new goal: "I want to start, because it's more fun to *play* with my friends than sit on the bench with them."

Making the World Better, One Cookie at a Time

Thirteen-year-old twins **Emma** and **Amy** are making a difference in the lives of others—and they started doing so when
they were just kids. Back when the twins were seven years
old, Emma saw a TV show about child entrepreneurs and
realized for the first time that *kids* could start businesses!
"I asked my mom if Amy and I could start one, and she said,
'Sure, you can do anything you want,'" says Emma. "She also
suggested that we do something to benefit others."

Soon after that, the twins went to a summer cooking
camp. That's when they got the idea of giving families living
in a nearby homeless shelter everything they needed to bake
oatmeal-chocolate-chip cookies. The girls were already familiar with the shelter. They had been using their birthday party
each year to collect items for the families living there. The
girls thought that those families, like their own, would enjoy
baking and bonding in the kitchen.

Thanks to a lot of hard work by the girls and their mom,
their simple idea of doing something nice for others has grown
into Bake Me Home (bakemehome.org), a charitable organization that brings together thousands of volunteers to help
families in homeless shelters, kids in foster care, and members
of the military. The organization also supports several food
pantries in the Cincinnati area where the girls live.

The girls began by spending a lot of time in their family's
kitchen with one goal in mind—to perfect their cookie recipe.
Once they did that, they set other goals. One was to get more
kids involved with their project, and another was to find a
church kitchen where those kids could come together to help.
And when it became clear that Bake Me Home needed more
space? The girls set a new goal of finding a building that Bake
Me Home could call its home. After a lot of fundraising, they
reached their goal and moved into that building.

Now the girls have other goals. Some are still related to
Bake Me Home, but others are more personal: get good grades,
go to college, find satisfying careers. Along the way, the girls
plan to keep using the goal-getting skills they've already
learned.

"A lot of people have grand plans and make unrealistic goals they can't keep," says Emma. "Then they feel like they failed. I think it's better to start small. With small goals, you may think you're not going to accomplish much, but those goals can grow into something bigger. That's what happened to us. We just wanted to give out some cookies. We didn't know it was going to grow into a big thing."

YOUR GOAL TRACKER

Now that you know some basics of goal setting—plus a few myths and truths about goals—are you ready to get goaling? First you'll need one important tool: a Goal Tracker. I suggest a blank book, spiral notebook, sketchpad, or three-ring binder—anything that gets you writing on paper and can be stored in a safe place.

Why is it important to use a paper Goal Tracker? Because writing (or drawing) by hand helps you get in touch with what's in your heart, not just your head. Writing also helps you clarify your thinking—and your goals. I recommend a subject notebook with dividers and pockets for extra storage, but use whatever works best for you. And if you find paper really isn't your style, you can use a phone, tablet, or computer.

Once you have your Goal Tracker, create two sections. Title the first section "Goal Keeper." Keep the forms that you print, copy, or scan here. Even if you're skeptical about the forms at first, I encourage you to give them a try. They're specially designed to help you get in touch with your dreams, clarify your goals, and keep you moving forward.

Title the second section of your Goal Tracker "Think

Hot Tip

Remember, even if it might seem easiest and quickest to just write straight on the forms in this book, resist that urge! If you download or copy these forms, you'll be able to get more out of this book in the long run.

It & Ink It." This will be your "thought log" for recording your answers to the "Think It & Ink It" exercises you'll find throughout this book. Also use this section to record other thoughts, memories, and reflections as you follow your dreams and pursue your goals. Lots of young people (and plenty of adults, too, including Ann Bancroft, filmmaker Guillermo del Toro, and Major Leaguer Daniel Norris) put pen to paper to help them get in touch with their thoughts, track their experiences, and explore what's happening in their lives. Journaling is also a great way to get to know yourself better. You can use your Think It & Ink It log to write about:

- ✔ why a particular goal has meaning for you
- ✔ how you felt before and after taking action
- ✔ problems you're facing and how you could handle them
- ✔ ideas and feelings you want to keep to yourself
- ✔ anything else that's on your mind

Here's what some teens have to say about their thought logs:

"When I feel like I'm bottling up my thoughts and feelings and need to get them out, I write about them."
—Alexus, 13

"I write my goals in big, bold letters. Then, I usually write how my day went, how I can improve, and what I need to keep working on." —Wai Wai, 13

"I capture ideas, images, and emotions that I can pour into the song lyrics I write." —Mary, 16

"I draw a lot, especially album covers." —Carson, 15

Everything in your Goal Tracker, including your Goal Keeper and your Think It & Ink It log, is private. That means you have total freedom to scribble, doodle, express ideas, write random thoughts, rant and rave, or do whatever else you're in the mood for. You can be messy or neat. And you can tear out any pages you don't feel like keeping. Don't worry about spelling, grammar, punctuation, or other details that might slow you down. The purpose of your Goal Tracker is to help you keep track of your goals and give you a safe place to express yourself in a way that works for you. No one else ever has to read what you write (unless you ask them to).

Once you've started your Goal Tracker, use these tips to get the most out of it:

1. **Date your entries.** Dates give you reference points to help you track your progress. When you look back—whether that's four weeks or four years from now—you'll be amazed to see how much you've accomplished.

2. **Use it often.** The more you use your Goal Tracker, the more you'll get out of it. You can write in it once a week, every few days, or every day.

3. **Create an "ideas" page.** Jot down things you want to learn more about, questions you want to ask others, and ideas for activities you'd like to try.

4. **Review it every few weeks.** Look back at what you wrote down weeks ago. It may take on new meaning in light of what you're doing today. And what you write today might help you solve a problem next week.

5. **Be creative.** Personalize your Goal Tracker with photos, drawings, quotes, or whatever else will make it meaningful to you.

If you're not sure a Goal Tracker will help you, test it out for a few weeks. You may discover that writing, drawing, recording, and imagining can give you insight into what you really want—insight you couldn't get any other way. Regularly putting pen to paper can also keep you focused on your goals. So give it try!

PART 2

DISCOVER
WHAT YOU
REALLY
WANT

WHAT ARE YOUR DREAMS?

"It's the possibility of having a dream come true that makes life interesting." —Paulo Coelho, novelist

Every day, you're bombarded with messages telling you what you should want and who you should be. Family, friends, teachers, the Internet, TV, magazines, radio, and billboards offer plenty of "advice." Do this. Say that. Own this. Wear that. Many people go through life listening too closely to these messages, often forgetting that the most meaningful hopes and dreams don't come from outside sources—they come from within.

Exploring your hopes and dreams—even the ones that seem out of reach—helps you begin to design the future you want. Ask yourself, "What do I really want?" Then listen to what you have to say.

Do I want to be a person known for helping others? For being trustworthy? For being adventurous? Do I want to stand up more strongly for myself and other people? Handle my feelings better? Try new things? Do I want to be an honor roll student, a baseball player, an artist, or an engineer? Do I want to try out for the school play, start a new club, or spend more time at home? Do I want to quit a sport, stop talking behind my friends' backs, or say no to junk food?

This conversation with yourself may be the most important (and challenging) one you'll ever have. So be sure to take some time to think about what's right for you.

Maybe you've got an answer right away: *I want to be a rock star . . . I want to see the world . . . I want to find a cure for diabetes . . . I want to scuba dive . . . I want to do well in school . . . I want to say no (or yes!) more often.* Or maybe you don't have any answers at all. Either way, it's time to dig a little deeper—to find out what you want, and why.

That's what Part 2 of this book is all about: daring to dream. You'll explore your hopes and desires—the ones you talk about, the ones you joke about, the ones you keep secret (even from yourself), and the ones you haven't yet discovered. That's why this section is called "Discover What You Really Want." It's not about what your parents, teachers, or coaches want for you. It's not about what your friends want for you. It's not about what advertisers or the media want for you. It's all about what *you* want—today, tomorrow, and for years to come.

To get started, answer the questions on Form #1, "What Inspires Me?" on page 31, and add the form to the Goal Keeper section of your Goal Tracker. The questions will help you identify and understand your sources of real inspiration.

DREAM STARTERS

On pages 32–33, you'll find Form #2, "Dream Starters." It features questions to help you start thinking about what you really want for yourself and your future. Fill in all five of the Dream Starters, or just choose the ones that capture your imagination. Keep your answers to yourself, or share them with your friends. You may also want to ask friends to answer the questions for themselves and share their answers with you.

THINK IT & INK IT

What are your talents and your strengths? Think about them and what you like to do. How might your talents and strengths become part of your future? Log your thoughts in the Think It & Ink It section of your Goal Tracker.

TWENTY BY TWENTY

"You have to dream before your dreams can come true." —A.P.J. Abdul Kalam, scientist and former president of India

Now that you've gotten in touch with some of your dreams, it's time to create what I call a "Twenty by Twenty" list. Print, copy, or scan Form #3 on pages 34–35 for the Goal Keeper section of your Goal Tracker, and then start listing the things you'd like to one day be, do, or have. Write as quickly as you can for five minutes or so.

Try to come up with at least ten ideas. Write down whatever crosses your mind, without worrying about how you'll accomplish it. Instead, imagine you have an endless supply of whatever you need—time, talent, money, motivation, and help from others. Don't be concerned if your ideas seem silly, out of reach, or even wildly extravagant. And don't short-change yourself by thinking too small.

In fact, this is the perfect time to try my "add two zeros" approach to dream making. Like turning 1 into 100, it's a way of amping up your dreams so that they could inspire not only your ten-year-old self (who may have had limited skills and resources), but also one-hundred-year-old you (who will have skills and resources you can't even imagine today). And even if your dreams seem nearly impossible right now, take to heart the words of thirteen-year-old Wai Wai, who has already achieved many of his dreams and has set his sights on more: "No dream is too big when you stayed focused on what matters."

Ordinary dream:	**"Add two zeros" dream:**
Visit three different countries.	Visit three different countries—on three different continents.
Go to college.	Earn a scholarship so I can afford to go to the college of my choice.
Have a clean room.	Build a robot that will keep my whole home clean for the rest of my life.
Get better at video games.	Get hired to travel around the world to teach kids how to play video games.

If you're having trouble getting in touch with your dreams, see pages 19–20 for some real-life dreams of other people.

THINK IT & INK IT

When you were younger, what were some of your hopes and dreams? How have your hopes and dreams changed in the past two years? In the past six months? How have *you* changed? How do you think you'll change in the next two years? The next ten years? How will these changes make it easier to go after your dreams? If some changes *won't* make it easier, what can you do about that? Write your answers in the Think It & Ink It section of your Goal Tracker.

GOAL GETTERS AND THEIR DREAMS

> "The best way to make your dreams come true is to wake up." —Paul Valéry, poet, essayist, and philosopher

Here's how some Goal Getters describe their dreams:

I want to . . .

"Travel around the world and help people." —Leela, 11

"Go skydiving." —Jenna, 16

"Get better at doing magic tricks and learn cooler tricks." —John, 13

"Complete a twisting flyaway backflip by the end of gymnastics season." —Abby, 17

"Get all my homework done the night it's assigned." —Betsy, 13

"Learn how to make *pâté*." —Max, 12

"Get into an advanced math class." —Marion, 11

"Get a job flying drones to record our high school football games." —Soren, 13

"Hit a home run." —Noah, 10

"Get along better with my sister." —Chris, 12

"Move to Argentina for a year and learn to speak Spanish." —Elena, 17

"Save $7,000 to pay for my first year of college." —Jordyn, 17

Do any of these dreams resemble yours? Or are they completely different? Which get you thinking in new directions? Which do you want to add to your Twenty by Twenty?

When you're done with your Twenty by Twenty list, talk with your friends about what you wrote and encourage them to make their own lists. Then, share what you wrote with one another (if you feel comfortable doing so). This is a great way to be inspired by your friends and their dreams—and to inspire them with yours. It's also a time when it's okay to steal: If one of your friends writes down something that makes you say, "Oh, I'd like to do that," or "Gosh, I'd be good at that," add it to your list—and keep on adding!

Still need more inspiration? Turn to Form #4, "Conversations Starters: What Are Your Dreams?" on pages 36–37, and use

Hot Tip

Use your Goal Tracker to start a "bucket list." A bucket list is a list of things you want to be, do, accomplish, or try in your lifetime. Sixteen-year-old Mary keeps hers on her phone. "My bucket list includes super extravagant things like traveling to India and backpacking across Europe," says Mary. "It also includes simpler things like visiting a nearby quarry and getting all A's this quarter. Every now and then, I look through the list, and ask myself what I could do to get closer to my goals."

the questions to check in with others about their dreams. You may be surprised by what you learn, so use the space provided to take notes. You can even use your phone or other device to record your conversations.

UNDERSTANDING YOUR VALUES

"Trust yourself. Think for yourself. Act for yourself. Speak for yourself. Be yourself." —Marva Collins, educator

In addition to being a place to explore your dreams and ideas, the "Dream Starters" and "Twenty by Twenty" forms can help you understand your values—what you believe in and what's most important to you deep down. Even if you're not aware of your values, they play a big part in who you are and what you want. They also play a big part in what inspires you. When you tune in to your values, they can become a guiding force for how you live your life.

Take another look at your completed forms, especially "Dream Starters," to see if you can begin to identify what you value. For example, suppose you wrote something like this for Dream Starter #2:

"NFL quarterback Russell Wilson is one of my heroes. He really believes in himself. As a kid, people told him he was too short to play football. But that didn't stop him. And even though he's the shortest starting quarterback in the NFL— only five feet, eleven inches—he helped his team win the Super Bowl. He does other cool things, too. For instance, he visits sick kids in the hospital and raises money for the Boys and Girls Clubs of America."

What might this passage say about you, your dreams, and your values?

On the surface, it could say that you enjoy sports, admire amazing athletic feats, and perhaps even dream of being a successful athlete yourself. But if you dig deeper, you might notice that you respect people who have a strong sense of self—who believe in themselves, even when the odds (and popular opinion) are against them. This might show that you value self-esteem, self-respect, hard work, and the ability to take healthy risks. Your answer could also reveal that you care about other people and want to help them.

Nearly every choice you make is influenced by your values. What you believe in (or don't believe in) helps you decide how to spend your time, who to spend it with, and how much energy to put into your activities. If you value having a close family, you'll be there for your parents and siblings when they need you. If you value helping your community, you'll volunteer. If you value being good at something (rapping, drawing, rock climbing, fixing cars), you'll make time to practice. In this way, values help guide how you live your life.

Some of your values might express a connection you have to other people or things such as:

✔ family	✔ faith or spirituality
✔ friends	✔ your culture
✔ education	✔ sports
✔ community	✔ music
✔ animals	✔ art
✔ the environment	✔ learning

Some of your values might express the kind of person you'd like to be or the way you'd like others to see you:

✔ kind	✔ loyal
✔ hardworking	✔ healthy
✔ capable	✔ independent
✔ loving	✔ creative
✔ helpful	
✔ honest	
✔ dependable	

To identify some of your values, review what you wrote on the "What Inspires Me," "Dream Starters," and "Twenty by Twenty" forms. Now ask yourself: *Who or what do I really care about? What holds meaning for me?*

Within the answers to these questions are your values. And these values are, in part, what drive your dreams. Here's what some teens have to say about their values:

"I value effort and loyalty." —Zack, 14

"I value being friendly, so I try to smile and say hi to everyone. And if I see someone having a bad day, I ask, 'What's up?'" —Alec, 15

"My values include caring for people and not being rude." —Kelsey, 13

"I value trying new things, so I tried out for hockey. I didn't make the team, but I'm happy I tried." —Betsy, 13

"My favorite character trait is my perseverance. Even if I'm really bad at something, I never give up." —Nick, 17

"I read more books than most kids in my class, and I'm the only one who auditioned for the school talent show, but I really like who I am, even if some kids make fun of me." —David, 12

"One of the hardest things I've done was standing up to one of my best friends who was bullying other people. I lost my friendship with her, but it was worth it." —Anna, 14

Do some of these values seem similar to yours? Does reading them help you identify what you believe in and what holds meaning for you?

You can use Form #5, "Values That Matter to Me," on pages 38–39 to learn more about yourself and your values. Store it in the Goal Keeper section of your Goal Tracker so you can refer to it often.

THINK IT & INK IT

How do your values differ from those of your friends? How are they the same? What are some ways your friends support your values and help you get what you want? Do any friends hold you back or make fun of you? If so, how do you feel about it, and what can you do about it? Explore these questions in the Think It & Ink It section of your Goal Tracker. Then, with your values in mind, write a "Code of Conduct" describing how you'd like to live your life. For example, if you value being friendly and caring, your Code of Conduct might include the following:

- Smile and say "Good morning" to my family every day.

- Ask my friends if they need help with their homework or a ride to practice.

- Be kind to all people and animals.

LET YOUR VALUES GUIDE YOUR DREAMS

"Values are like fingerprints. Nobody's are the same, but you leave them all over everything you do." —Elvis Presley, singer and actor

Your values form the foundation of your life. They also form the foundation of your dreams. And just as each person's values are unique, so are each person's dreams. Take Kylie and Shauna, who are profiled in the next Goal Getters in Action. They are both caring individuals who value making a difference. However, Kylie, a cancer survivor, dreams of helping kids with cancer, while Shauna wants to help girls around the world and dreams of becoming president of the United States.

GOAL GETTERS iN ACTioN

A Backpack That Gives Back

Twelve-year-old **Kylie**, from Naugatuck, Connecticut, knows what it's like to set goals that support her values. When she was just eight, she was diagnosed with cancer. She had to have forty-six weeks of chemotherapy and radiation. While in the hospital, she could move around, but she hated having to lug her IV pole. It was heavy and awkward, and Kylie often tripped over the pole's tubes.

So several years later, when her fifth-grade science class was instructed to invent something that solved a problem, Kylie knew immediately what she wanted to do. Her goal was to invent something that made it easier for kids having chemo to move around. That something turned out to be a backpack that Kylie, with her parents' help, outfitted with a battery-powered controller to regulate chemo flow, and a small wire cage to protect the chemo bag.

Some of Kylie's teachers saw the value in her special backpack, and submitted it to the Connecticut Invention Convention, where it won. Since then, people from all over the United States have contributed over $50,000 dollars to Kylie's fundraising campaign. The money is being used to produce the backpack, and Kylie couldn't be more excited to see her goal become real.

"I feel like I can do anything now," says Kylie. And what does she most want to do? Help others. "I want to donate my backpack to hospitals and camps for kids with cancer, and I want to be able to visit all the kids and see them smile," says Kylie.

Go-for-the-Goal Pals

Sixteen-year-old **Shauna** lives in New York City, yet her generous spirit extends around the world. "I've always been really interested in global issues, especially involving women's rights," says Shauna. So just before tenth grade, she talked her friends into starting a local chapter of Girl Effect. It's an international organization dedicated to the belief that girls play a crucial role in solving some of the world's most persistent problems.

Contributing to Girl Effect's work was a way for Shauna to align her actions with her values, which include making a difference in the lives of others. That's something Shauna has wanted to do for as long as she can remember. It's also one of the reasons she plans to study international relations when she gets to college.

So far, Shauna and the Girl Effect chapter she helped establish have raised more than $5,000 by working at school events, holding bake sales, and organizing other activities. The chapter plans to send the money to Bangladesh so that forty girls there can start their own club. Shauna says, "Just think, three friends in a New York living room made a decision, and now, eighteen months later, we're helping improve the lives of girls halfway around the world. It shows that everyone can do something."

GET YOUR DREAM ON!

To think more specifically about your values and dreams, turn on your favorite music, close your eyes, and ask yourself *exactly* what you want in your life—now and in the future. If you were given the opportunity to do or have anything, what would it be, and why?

Think about what you can accomplish relatively quickly, such as unloading the dishwasher, finishing a history report, or completing a job application. Next consider things that might take a little longer, either because they require more work or because they won't happen until you're older, such as trying out for next spring's play, qualifying for a college scholarship, or buying your first car. Finally, think about things that will require even more time to make happen, such as producing your first album, becoming a paleontologist, or starting a family. Finally, imagine your biggest goals of all, even if they seem almost impossible now—like competing in the Olympics or becoming a translator for the United Nations. While goals such as these may seem out of reach today, they won't always feel that way.

YOUR DREAM BOARD

> "Your imagination is your preview of life's coming attractions." —Albert Einstein, physicist

Another way to get in touch with your dreams and make them more real is to create a Dream Board. A Dream Board is a collection of pictures, words, images, and objects related to your hopes, dreams, and values. It allows you to think in pictures instead of words. It's your own personal work of art that represents all the things you'd like to do with your life. Like a blueprint that puts an architect's dream on paper—where everyone can see it—your Dream Board will help make your dreams more real by turning them into something you can see and touch.

You'll need:

- ✔ magazines, catalogs, brochures, and other printed materials with lots of pictures you can cut out

- ✔ small objects related to your dreams such as maps, theater tickets, a guitar pick, or a ski pass

- ✔ one or more photographs or drawings of yourself

- ✔ scissors

- ✔ glue, rubber cement, or tape

- ✔ poster board or other heavy paper

1. Cut out pictures from the magazines, catalogs, brochures, and other printed materials of things you'd like to be, do, or have at some point in your life. Also cut out pictures of people or things that represent the values you want

to have. For instance, if you dream of being a writer, cut out a picture of your favorite author. If you value perseverance, find a photo of someone who has overcome big challenges.

2. Look for words, captions, quotes, and phrases that reflect characteristics you'd like to possess (bravery, intelligence, curiosity) or your philosophy on life (better the world, continue to learn, be kind to animals).

3. Sort through the images, words, and objects you've collected, and set aside any that don't represent your true dreams and values.

4. Now assemble your Dream Board. Put a picture of yourself in the center of the poster board or paper. Arrange images, words, and objects around your picture however you like, and then glue or tape them in place.

5. Put your finished Dream Board where you'll see it when you wake up and before you go to sleep. You can also take a photo of your Dream Board or make a smaller version to store in your Goal Tracker, hang in your locker, tape to the bathroom mirror, or carry in your backpack, so you'll always be reminded of your dreams.

"I have a big collage in my room of all the goals I want to achieve someday." —Wai Wai, 13

"I make collages all the time. I include people who inspire me and people I want to be like. I also include quotes and other things that motivate me." —Anna, 14

"I'm really into swimming so I cut out pictures of a bunch of swimmers and swimming pools to make a collage." —Kelsey, 13

GoAL GETTERS iN ACTioN

Bump, Set, Spike: Score!

Fourteen-year-old **Meredith** fell in love with volleyball in sixth grade, when she tried out for and made her school's team. That's when she created a Dream Board that included volleyball-related goals. At first, they were simple: touch a volleyball every day and learn how to serve the ball over the net. As her skills and confidence grew, so did her goals. By the time she entered ninth grade, her goal was to make the junior varsity team.

Despite going to summer camps and practicing at school, her local gym, and in the garage with her mom (a former volleyball player), Meredith only made C-Squad. She was crushed, but kept working hard. "I thought maybe the coach would see my effort and pull me up to JV," says Meredith. Before long, that's exactly what happened. "At first I just practiced with the JV team," explains Meredith. "Finally, just before the first game of the season, my coach told me to dress for JV. I was so excited."

Meredith's excitement grew when she was put into the game. "I played the best game of my life," says Meredith. "All the hard work was totally worth it because I showed that I really did belong on the team." Her coach agreed. "At our next practice, in front of everybody, he announced that he was pulling me up to JV full time. That was my goal, and I achieved it!"

THINK IT & INK IT

Fast forward. Imagine it's 2050 and you've just achieved the very thing you've dreamed of for many years. Use the Think It & Ink It section of your Goal Tracker to write a letter to yourself at whatever age you are now. In this letter, offer yourself advice and encouragement.

YOU'RE ON YOUR WAY

"Only you can control your future." —Dr. Seuss, children's book writer and illustrator

Now that you've written down your dreams and values, and made a Dream Board, you're on your way toward creating a better future for yourself. But don't stop now. Keep on dreaming! As you identify new dreams, write about them in your Goal Tracker, and add them to your "Twenty by Twenty" list and your Dream Board. The more you do so, the more your motivation will grow and the clearer your path will become. Now it's time to get goaling!

Form #1   Date: _____

 Add to your Goal Tracker!

WHAT INSPIRES ME?

What do I enjoy doing? Why?

What don't I enjoy doing? Why not?

What gives meaning and purpose to my life?

What are my talents or skills? How might I improve them?

What do I like to read or watch movies about?

What do I daydream about?

Add to your
Goal Tracker!

DREAM STARTERS

Dream Starter #1: Write about three people you know personally and admire. They can be friends, family members, teachers, coaches, neighbors, or anyone else. What do they do that you think is great? What makes them special to you?

Dream Starter #2: Write about three people you admire but haven't met—for example, celebrities, leaders, athletes, artists, or historical figures. What have they done that you think is great? What makes them special to you?

Dream Starter #3: Fast forward to graduation night. Just before you head into the auditorium, you're asked to make five predictions about what you expect to one day accomplish or become. What do you predict? Add as many details as you can.

Dream Starter #4: Imagine you're about to attend your five-year high school reunion. You've been asked to make a three-minute video about your life. List the events and accomplishments you'll highlight. Why did you choose these things?

Dream Starter #5: Imagine you're turning seventy, and your friends are about to honor you with a Lifetime Achievement Award. What will they say about you? What have you done that they (and you) think is special? Did you go to college? Create art? Become a star? Start a business? Were you generous to your friends? A good parent? Fun to be around? A thoughtful listener? Committed to a cause?

Add to your
Goal Tracker!

TWENTY BY TWENTY

If you could do any twenty things by the time you turn
twenty, what would they be?

1.

2.

3.

4.

5.

6.

7.

8.

9.

➡

Form #3 continued . . .

10.

11.

12.

13.

14.

15.

16.

17.

18.

19.

20.

CONVERSATiON STARTERS:
WHAT ARE YOUR DREAMS?

*Ask these questions of friends, family members, or other people
in your life.*

If you could do anything, what would it be? Why?

What's the first thing you remember really, *really* wanting to
do? Have you done it? Why or why not?

What matters to you more than anything else?

➡

Form #4 continued . . .

What are some of your hopes and dreams?

What really inspires you?

What could you imagine *me* growing up to be or do?

Add to your
Goal Tracker!

VALUES THAT MATTER TO ME

Take a few moments to check in with your values. Begin by
naming some people and things you feel strongly connected to.

Next, pick three of these to write about. Ask yourself: Why do
I feel connected to this person or thing?

1.

2.

3.

Think about the personal qualities that are important to you. Write about them and how you can demonstrate them.

Review what you've written so far, and look over the list of values on page 22. Then, list three values important to you. Remember, your values are the ideas or things that matter most to you.

1.

2.

3.

PART 3

BECOME A GOAL GETTER

THE LONG AND SHORT OF GOALS

> "Sometimes you gotta create what you want to be part of." —Geri Weitzman, psychologist

In "Part 2: Discover What You Really Want," you found ways to unleash your hopes and dreams. Now, how do you go from where you are today to a tomorrow where those hopes and dreams become reality?

By taking action.

Sure, it would be nice if simply dreaming about or hoping for something would lead to a better future, but life doesn't work that way. It's up to you to make your dreams real. This is where goal setting comes in. Your goals are the "how-to" process for reaching your dreams.

Some goals, such as taking your younger sister to a movie, writing a history report, or reading all the books in your favorite series, can be achieved in a day, a week, or a month. These are called short-term goals. Others, such as being named MVP on next season's tennis team, graduating from college, or becoming fluent in another language, require much more time, effort, and commitment. These are long-term goals.

 **Hot Tip**

Don't be tempted to set *only* short-term goals. Having long-term goals is really important—even if you have to work longer and harder to achieve them. That's because long-term goals improve short-term decision-making. Think about it: Say you're a seventh-grader whose long-term goal is earning a college scholarship so you can study engineering. To earn a scholarship, you know you need good grades. To get good grades, you know you need to study hard now so you can learn a lot, especially in math. You have a math test tomorrow. So tonight, what do you do? Instead of goofing off, you spend thirty minutes solving math problems. This short-term decision gets you one step closer to your long-term goal.

Usually, long-term goals are broken down into several short-term goals that help you keep moving forward. In this sense, short-term goals support your long-term goals. But short-term goals don't always have to lead up to long-term ones. Some can stand alone, like finishing your homework by the time your friends come over, or getting along with your family for the entire day.

Setting and reaching small, stand-alone goals like these can get you in a goal-setting frame of mind and help you build your goal-setting muscles. And once you prove to yourself that you really can reach your goals, you'll feel inspired to take on more challenging goals that require more time (and effort) to complete.

GOAL GETTERS iN ACTioN

A Goal That's Out of This World

"Ever since I was little, I wanted to be an astronaut," says seventeen-year-old **Abby**. "Even more than that, I've wanted to go to Mars." And while getting to Mars may be a distant dream for most people, to Abby it's a well-defined long-term goal that she's been working toward for years. To prepare herself mentally, she takes classes at a local university. To prepare physically, she competes in swimming, diving, and gymnastics.

Practice Pays Off

Last baseball season, twelve-year-old **David** had a goal: to throw from the back of right field all the way to second base without anybody in the middle. Says David: "Not a lot of people believed in me, but I practiced and practiced, and then in one of our last games of the season, somebody hit a ball over our right-fielder's head. So I ran, picked up the ball, and threw it to second base. I had to play catch a lot to make that throw, but it was worth it."

GET SMART: SAVVY, MEASURABLE, ACTIVE, REACHABLE, TIMED

> "If you don't know where you are going, you might wind up someplace else." —Yogi Berra, former baseball player, coach, and manager

Labeling your goals as short-term or long-term isn't the most important thing you'll need to know about setting goals. What's more important is that your goals be SMART. What that means is that the goals you set—whether they're short-term or long-term—need to be:

Savvy

Measurable

Active

Reachable

Timed

Savvy goals are easy to understand and use. They're the opposite of goals that are vague, confusing, or difficult to follow. They're also the opposite of goals that aren't your own. To make your goals savvy, keep them both personal (meaningful to you and aligned with your values) and positive (so you feel good about what you're trying to accomplish). After all, it's easier to get excited about a positive goal you believe in (learn to play the bass) than a negative one (stop exceeding my monthly download limit), or one that someone else wants *for* you.

"Construct *my dream house* out of paper and tape."
—Amy, 13

Measurable goals define exactly what you intend to accomplish. Play a video game for thirty minutes, study for one hour, and walk one mile are all examples of measurable goals that make your destination crystal clear. To make your goals measurable, get as specific as possible about the outcome you want.

 "Shoot *1,000 pucks a week.*" —Avery, 12

Active goals tell you what specific action to take. They feature "do it" words, or verbs, such as "sail," "sing," or "ski." Strong and specific, these words and others like them keep you moving forward. They also make your actions visible. They help you *see* yourself sailing, singing, or skiing, which means you (and others) will know you're working toward your goal.

 "*Run* a marathon." —Betsy, 13

Reachable goals stretch you, but not beyond your limits. They require work—sometimes hard work—but they can be reached. To check if a goal is reachable for *you*—not for your best friend, older brother, or someone you admire from afar—look at where you are today (I have $14 saved) and ask yourself, "Is this goal (saving $75) realistic for me?" Also ask, "Is this goal enough of a challenge?" Goals that are too easy can quickly fade away.

 "Even though my sister's had a perfect GPA all her life, *my goal* is to get As and Bs." —Anna, 14

Timed goals have clear deadlines: times or dates by which you'll be able to say, "I did it!" These deadlines (at 7 p.m., on Wednesday, before school starts, by my birthday) give you a target to aim for. They also motivate you—kind of like school assignment due dates.

 "Learn all my lines for the school play *by next Friday.*" —Alexus, 13

From Not-So-SMART to SMART

When you're first learning how to set SMART goals, you might stumble and end up with some not-so-SMART goals. That's okay! Because you can turn those not-so-SMART goals into SMART ones. Here's how:

Not-so-SMART goal:	Why it's not-so-SMART and what to do about it:	SMART goal:
"Try not to look like a loser on the basketball court so Dad doesn't get mad."	No one wants to look like a loser, but this goal isn't very *savvy*. It's not likely to ignite your passion, it's not positive, and it's not personal. Doing well because it matters to your dad isn't the same as doing well because it matters to *you*. Tap into your values and set a goal that's meaningful to you.	"Turn up the tunes and get Dad to practice jump shots with me for twenty minutes three times a week so I can start at least one game this upcoming basketball season."
"Get healthier."	This is a nice idea, but not a very *measurable* goal. Why? Because the outcome you want to achieve isn't clear. Does getting "health-ier" mean eating breakfast every morning, walking to school instead of riding the bus, or flossing your teeth before bed? Smarten up this goal by making what you want to accomplish crystal clear.	"Sleep at least eight hours every night (except when I have sleepovers or am out of town with my family)."
"Be a better person."	Being a better person is a wor-thy aim, but there's no clear "do it" word in this goal. What action might you take to "be better"? Keep your desk organized, talk more in class, volunteer at a shelter for homeless families? Make this and all of your goals *active* by including strong action verbs that move you forward.	"Volunteer to tutor kids at the library for at least two hours every week."

"Get an A+ in chemistry."	Is this goal truly *reachable* for you? Perhaps—if you're already close to an A (and if your school's grading curve includes A+). But what if you're struggling to understand the material? A more reachable goal may be aiming for a B, or scheduling several tutoring sessions.	"Form a chemistry study group by next weekend and meet twice a week for the rest of the semester to study."
"Buy a new bike."	This goal isn't clearly *timed*. Just as you're more likely to work on a school assignment that has a specific due date, you're more likely to work on a goal that has a clear deadline. Like goals themselves, deadlines should be specific. "By May 31, 2020" leaves no doubt as to when you intend to complete your goal.	"Buy a new bike before my next birthday."

To remind yourself of what SMART goals are, print, copy, or scan Form #6, "SMART Card," on page 60 and keep it in the Goal Keeper section of your Goal Tracker. You can also cut out the card, decorate and laminate it, and use it as a bookmark or carry it in your wallet. You can even take a picture of it and use it as your phone's screensaver.

THINK IT & INK IT

Have you ever set a not-so-SMART goal? If so, how did you feel about it? What did you learn from the experience? Is there a way you could have revised your goal so that it *was* SMART? If it's a goal you're still interested in, revise it now and write down three things you could do in the next week to help move you forward. Use the Think It & Ink It section of your Goal Tracker.

GOALS COME IN ALL SHAPES AND SIZES

> "A good goal is like a strenuous exercise—it makes you stretch." —Mary Kay Ash, business owner

The term "one-size-fits-all" hardly ever applies to goals. That's because no two people are alike. Your goals may be very different from your best friend's goals, even if the two of you have plenty of other things in common. The way you both approach your goals may vary a lot, too (even if you share the same goals). You may aim for lofty long-term goals, while your friend may shoot for simple short-term ones. Your goals—whether they're big, small, or somewhere in between—should be the right size for you.

Some Goal Getters find it helpful to divide their goals into categories, such as school, friends, sports, and so on. The following categories reflect some SMART goals that young people say are important to them. You may want to use these goals as inspiration for ones you can set in your own life. Of course, that doesn't mean you need to set goals in all of these areas—at least, not all at the same time. And you don't have to have more than one goal in any area. But these categories can help you think about what's important to you, and help you brainstorm ideas for goals you might want to set.

Personal

- ✔ Learn the definition of one new word each day.
- ✔ Set up a Pinterest account and learn how to use it by the end of the month.
- ✔ Play chess at least once each week.
- ✔ Read at least one book for fun each quarter.

School

- ✔ Improve my math grade this semester.
- ✔ Make the honor roll at least once each year while in high school.
- ✔ By September, find out which colleges offer degrees in architecture.
- ✔ Sign up for the peer tutoring program.

Friends

- ✔ Each time I ride the bus, say hi to three classmates.
- ✔ Send my friends homemade cards on their birthdays.
- ✔ Compliment two people every day about something other than how they look.
- ✔ Call my friend before practice to apologize for what I said at lunch.

Family

- ✔ Spend time with my grandparents at least once a month.
- ✔ Go to the park with my little brother every Wednesday afternoon.
- ✔ Willingly say yes when Dad asks me to do my chores.
- ✔ Come home before my curfew when I'm out with my friends.

Community

- ✔ Volunteer to usher at the upcoming school play.
- ✔ Each semester, give away the clothes I no longer wear.
- ✔ Shovel the sidewalks on my block.
- ✔ Donate books I no longer want to the library book drive.

Sports

- ✔ Make this year's lacrosse team.
- ✔ Get a personal best in the 100-yard dash.
- ✔ Keep track of how many minutes I practice each day.
- ✔ Try out for a sport I didn't play last year.

Work

- ✔ Apply for three summer jobs before school ends.
- ✔ By December 1, ask my boss for more hours.
- ✔ By Memorial Day, make and distribute a flyer to promote my lawn-raking business.
- ✔ By the end of the first week at my new job, find at least one person who can answer questions when I have them.

Money

- ✔ Open a bank account by the end of the month.
- ✔ Save $500 this summer for my college fund.
- ✔ Help Mom make a budget for a family vacation this spring.
- ✔ Each week, donate the price of one school lunch to a food bank.

Thinking of goals that fall into these categories is a good way to get some perspective on the different areas of your life—including what's working, what's not, and what could be improved. Here's something to remember, though: You don't have to work on every category at once. In fact, trying to tackle too much at one time could create a lot of unnecessary stress!

Instead, stay balanced by focusing on only one or two major areas at a time. And when pursuing your goals, be sure to leave room for other life essentials: sleep, friends, fun, and adventure! Also leave room for the unexpected. As you no doubt already know, even the most thoughtful plans can go awry when you're snowed in, rained out, or otherwise unable to do what you'd planned.

To put you in a well-balanced frame of mind, check out pages 68–69, where you'll find "Conversation Starters: What Are Your Goals?" You can also read these words of wisdom from Goal Getters who are managing the demands of a busy life:

"Sometimes, even if you think you did as much as you can, do a little more. Other times, do a little less. That way, you won't always feel stressed out." —Will, 12

"Knowing what my goals are helps me determine where to put my effort. That might mean working extra hard on an essay and racing through my Spanish assignment." —Hannah, 16

"I balance karate, which is mostly physical, with doing magic tricks, which is mostly mental." —John, 13

"When I see a grade in one subject start to slide and yet I'm achieving above and beyond in another subject, I try to even things out." —Elena, 17

THINK IT & INK IT

Think about the goal categories on pages 49–50 in relation to your own life. Is there a particular category that's stressing you out? If so, why? Are you trying to do too much in that area? Or have you been too busy in other areas to give it a second thought? Come up with five ideas for how you might be able to bring your goals more in balance. Write your ideas in the Think It & Ink It section of your Goal Tracker.

SET YOUR GOALS

> "Setting goals is the first step in turning the invisible into the visible." —Tony Robbins, author and motivational speaker

Now that you've gotten a better sense of the categories goals can fall into and an idea of the types of goals other people set, pull out your Goal Tracker and review the Goal Keeper pages you've filled out so far. Also look at the Think It & Ink It exercises you've completed, as well as anything else you've written in your Goal Tracker.

Taking a few minutes to review all the work you've done so far will reconnect you with your hopes and dreams, jumpstart your Goal Getter get-up-and-go, and prepare you to ask yourself this big question: What do I *really* want my goals to be?

Once you have an idea, complete Form #7, "What I Really Want," on page 61. Save the form in the Goal Keeper section of your Goal Tracker. That way, when you're ready to start on a new goal, you'll have a list to choose from.

If you still feel unsure of what you want, figure out what's blocking you. Do you doubt your ability to succeed? Do you feel that your mom, dad, or some other adult has unrealistic expectations of you that are getting in the way of your real goals? Do you feel like you don't deserve what you want? Are you worried about what your friends will think? Talking or writing about your feelings helps you understand them. Writing a letter to someone you trust (even if you never send it) can help, too.

Once you've had time to sort through your thoughts and feelings, you can start to change your circumstances if necessary. Here's some advice from one teen who did:

> "If you're doing something you really hate because your parents or someone else wants you to, you owe it to yourself to tell them how you feel." —Alexus, 13

While it's important to stay true to yourself when setting goals, don't restrict yourself so much that you never try anything new. The biggest regrets people have aren't about what they did, but what they didn't do. In fact, read the following Goal Getters in Action section, and you'll meet a few teens who fell in love with activities they never expected to enjoy (or be good at).

THINK IT & INK IT

In the Think It & Ink It section of your Goal Tracker, write for five minutes about the person you want to be, the life you want to live, and the things you want to do. If you get stuck and can't think of anything, just write "I want, I want" over and over until a new thought breaks through. Then ask yourself whether your wants are in line with your values. If they're not, spend a little more time thinking and inking about what you want and why.

GOAL GETTERS iN ACTiON

Karate Kid

Thirteen-year-old **John** knew nothing about karate, until a group of students from a local karate dojo showed up at his school to do a demo. "I thought it looked cool, so I asked my parents if I could give it a try," says John. Three years later, he's earned nine belts and is only six months away from his ultimate goal: his black belt.

Act Two

Shauna, age sixteen, fell in love with theater her freshman year. "I thought it was going to be my whole life, that it was my destiny," says Shauna. "But then, sophomore year, my parents talked me into trying track. I'm so glad they did. I discovered I really like being athletic. And now I have friends from both theater and track."

A Great Debate

Twelve-year-old **David** joined his school's speech and debate team, eager to present pro and con arguments on various topics. But on the first day of practice, his coach assigned him poems to read instead. Even though it wasn't what David had been expecting, he excelled, earning high rankings in his very first tournament.

YOUR "GOAL LADDER" ACTION PLAN

"To fail to plan is to plan to fail." —Benjamin Franklin, diplomat, author, and inventor

Imagine eating an apple all in one bite. That's what going for your goals can feel like if you don't first break them into bite-size pieces, which is exactly why experts advise having a step-by-step action plan, which I call a "Goal Ladder." Just as a real ladder helps you climb higher rung by rung, so does a Goal Ladder. Keep climbing, and you'll eventually reach your destination.

To build a Goal Ladder of your own, start with Form #8, "My Goal Ladder" on page 62. Print, copy, or scan this form for each of your goals and put it in your Goal Tracker. Then follow these five steps:

Step 1: Decide on a goal. Think about your short-term goals (what you want to accomplish in the next days, weeks, or months),

Hot Tip

Climbing your Goal Ladder is much easier when it's on a strong foundation, which happens when your goals match up with your values. To check on your ladder's foundation, take a look at what you wrote on the "Values That Matter to Me" form on pages 38–39. Is your chosen goal connected to your values? If not, revise it. Also take into account how much time and energy you have to devote to your goal. Given everything else on your plate, is now the right time to go for this goal?

as well as your long-term goals (what you want to accomplish two, ten, or twenty years from now). Review the "What I Really Want" form in the Goal Keeper section of your Goal Tracker. Then, choose one goal to work on.

Step 2: Write it down. Once you've chosen your goal, make sure it's SMART (Savvy, Measurable, Active, Reachable, and Timed). Revise it if it's not quite there yet. Then write it down on your "My Goal Ladder" form. The very act of writing your goal will help crystallize it in your mind.

Step 3: Brainstorm the steps. Brainstorm everything you'll need to do to reach the top of your Goal Ladder by asking, "What will it take to climb from one rung to the next?" You can write your action steps on a fresh page of your Goal Tracker or on the back of your copy of the "My Goal Ladder" form. Suppose, for example, that your SMART goal is to score higher than a B on your next history test. Your action steps might include:

- ✔ make a list of everything I need to study
- ✔ study
- ✔ ask someone to quiz me on the material
- ✔ attend a study group session (or two)
- ✔ take a practice test
- ✔ review each chapter of the unit
- ✔ organize my notes
- ✔ talk with my teacher about what's going to be on the test

Step 4: Fill in your Goal Ladder. Look over your action steps. Cross out any that don't seem useful, and combine those that are similar. Then rewrite the remaining steps in an order that seems logical to you. Your revised list might look like this:

- ✔ organize my notes
- ✔ begin review of each chapter

✔ attend study group sessions

✔ take a practice test

✔ study and ask someone to quiz me

Next, write your first action step on the first rung of your Goal Ladder. For sample Goal Ladders, turn to pages 64–66. Here you'll see ladders of different lengths and how they work. Use them to guide you as you arrange your action steps on your own Goal Ladder. As you do, keep in mind that there are no right or wrong answers when making a Goal Ladder. Just come up with the steps and an order that work for you.

When you're done filling in the steps, set a deadline for each, and write it alongside the appropriate rung. Some rungs may have a deadline like "Each night" or "After school every Monday." Others may have a deadline like "By next Tuesday" or "Before the end of year." Either is fine, as long as your deadlines feel manageable—not so tight that you feel squeezed by them, and not so far ahead that you forget about them. Your deadlines also shouldn't conflict with other activities or commitments, so if you haven't already done so, pull out your daily planner, class syllabus, game schedule, or family calendar for reference.

Step 5. Start climbing.

Don't wait! Get up right now and do one small thing that will move you closer to your goal: Pull out your

Hot Tip

When deciding how many action steps to have for your goals, ten is a good rule of thumb. That said, some goals will need fewer than ten rungs. Others—especially long-term goals—will need more. For these bigger goals, use Form #9, the "Extension Ladder," on page 63. But be sure your goal isn't so high that there's no end in sight. If you find yourself building a Goal Ladder that reaches to the moon, take some time to rethink your goal and figure out what you can reasonably achieve. Yet don't be so afraid of heights that you don't challenge yourself. Just as setting goals gets easier with practice, so does climbing your Goal Ladder.

history book, dig out your notes, or tape your syllabus above your desk. Completing small tasks such as these releases endorphins, the brain's "feel-good" chemical. Starting small also helps build motivation. Research shows that the most effective motivation is progress, and the surest way to make progress is by getting started.

"Think of something you want to do, and if it's something really big, think of a few small steps that will help you get there." —Zack, 14

Once you've completed your goal ladder:

✔ **Seal the deal.** Sign your name to your Goal Ladder. This agreement with yourself shows that you're serious about your goal.

✔ **Make it visible.** To keep your goal top of mind, put a copy of your Goal Ladder on your bulletin board, in your locker or backpack, under your pillow, and any-place else you'll see it often.

✔ **Spread the word.** You may want to show your Goal Ladder to your family and friends, so they know what you're setting out to accomplish.

THINK IT & INK IT

Imagine you've just climbed to the top of your Goal Ladder. You open the most recent issue of your school or community paper and see an article about you and what you've accomplished. In the Think It & Ink It section of your Goal Tracker, write the article you'd like to read. Explain the goal you set, what steps you took to reach it, why it was important to you, and how you feel now that you've achieved it. The article can be just a few sentences or several paragraphs. Or if you prefer, make a video of yourself talking about your accomplishments as though you're being interviewed.

GOAL GETTERS iN ACTiON

Climbing to the Top, One Rung at a Time

When thirteen-year-old **Wai Wai** was in sixth grade, he achieved his goal of becoming president of his elementary school. That's an impressive accomplishment for any kid, but it has extra meaning when you consider that Wai Wai didn't speak English when he and his family arrived in the United States from a Thai refugee camp five years earlier.

"People looked down on me sometimes because I didn't speak English well," Wai Wai confesses. "Some of my classmates said I'd *never* be able to. But I didn't listen. Instead, I told myself, 'If they say it's impossible, do the impossible.'"

That is exactly what Wai Wai has done. Today, he speaks English flawlessly. The key to his success? His Goal Ladder. Here are the rungs he climbed to reach his goal of becoming school president:

✔ Learn English.

✔ Improve my English and learn math.

✔ Get better in all my classes.

✔ Work on my leadership skills.

✔ Start giving speeches.

✔ Become school president and make the school better.

Thanks to his determination and hard work, including after-school tutoring four nights a week, Wai Wai climbed each rung of his Goal Ladder. Along the way, he overcame several obstacles. One was his temper. "At one time I wasn't a very good student, because I had anger issues," he says. "When people messed with me, I'd lose my temper." As a result, Wai Wai spent a lot of time in detention. "But I knew I had to stop getting angry so that I could be a good role model for other kids," says Wai Wai.

With support from his teachers, parents, and friends, Wai Wai learned to control his temper and channel his energy into

new goals, which include winning a state wrestling championship, earning a college scholarship, and becoming a leader in
his community.

Puppy Love

Ever since first grade, **Sky Li**, now a ninth-grader, has known
exactly what she really wants: to become a veterinarian. She's
steadily climbing her Goal Ladder toward this lifelong dream.

Her first goal was to get a dog. That took longer than
she hoped. "My mom thought my sister and I might not
be responsible enough," says Sky Li. So she started saving
money, putting aside birthday checks from her grandparents
into a Puppy Fund. She also focused on helping more around
the house, and getting along better with her younger sister.
Finally, when Sky Li was in sixth grade, she and her sister
welcomed Clover—a half lab, half cocker spaniel rescue dog—
to their family.

That's also when Sky Li began working toward the next
rung of her Goal Ladder: finding a way to work with animals.
Unlike her previous goal, this one happened more quickly
than she expected. One day, a routine trip to the vet for
Clover turned out to be anything *but* routine for Sky Li. The
clinic was short-staffed, and Sky Li (thanks to a bit of nudg-
ing from her mom), volunteered to help. Before long, she was
shadowing the veterinarians on school vacation days and over
the summer. "I've observed several procedures and surgeries,
developed X-rays, and once I pulled out a dog's tooth," she
says. "I was scared at first because I thought I might faint at
the sight of blood, but being able to see things firsthand has
actually made me even more excited about my goal of becoming a vet."

Add to your
Goal Tracker!

SMART CARD

My goals need to be:

Savvy (easy to understand and use)

Measurable (specific about what I plan to accomplish)

Active (clear about the action I need to take)

Reachable (within my reach)

Timed (complete with specific deadlines)

WHAT I REALLY WANT

Make a "Top Five List" of what you really want—not what others (parents, friends, teachers, the media) seem to want for you. Focus on what's truly meaningful to you. Write your "Top Fives" into sentences that start with the words "I really want." Then turn each "want" into a SMART goal.

My Top Fives	
I really want:	**My SMART goal is:**

MY GOAL LADDER

My goal: _____

My deadline: _____

My signature: _____

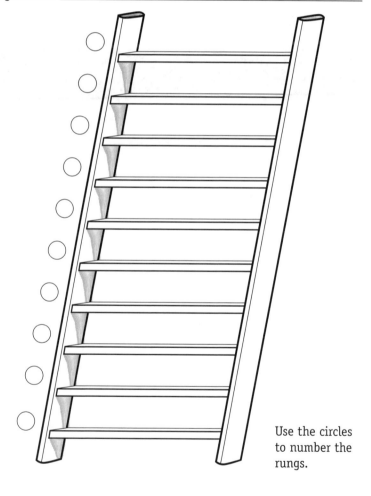

Use the circles
to number the
rungs.

EXTENSION LADDER

My goal: _____

My deadline: _____

My signature: _____

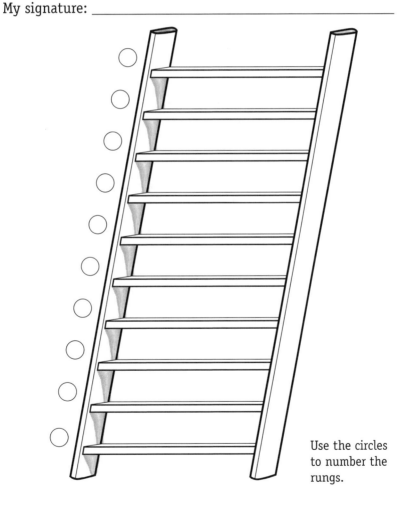

Use the circles
to number the
rungs.

SAMPLE GoAL LADDER

My goal: <u>Score higher than a 90 on my next history test.</u>

My deadline: <u>Test is March 3!</u>

My signature: <u>*Hector D.*</u>

This goal doesn't
need ten rungs.

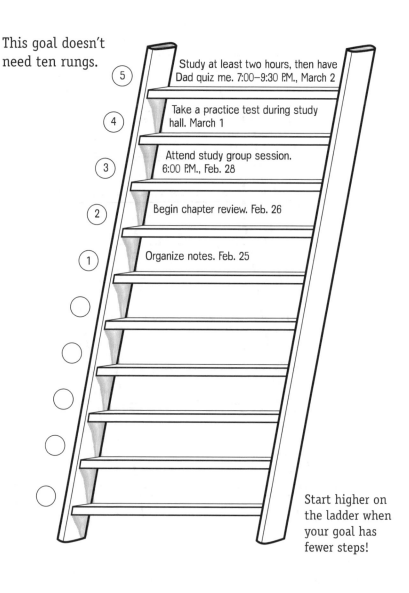

5 Study at least two hours, then have Dad quiz me. 7:00–9:30 P.M., March 2

4 Take a practice test during study hall. March 1

3 Attend study group session. 6:00 P.M., Feb. 28

2 Begin chapter review. Feb. 26

1 Organize notes. Feb. 25

Start higher on
the ladder when
your goal has
fewer steps!

SAMPLE GOAL LADDER

My goal: <u>Get a part-time job after school.</u>

My deadline: <u>By Nov. 15</u>

My signature: <u>*Mei L.*</u>

This goal uses all ten rungs.

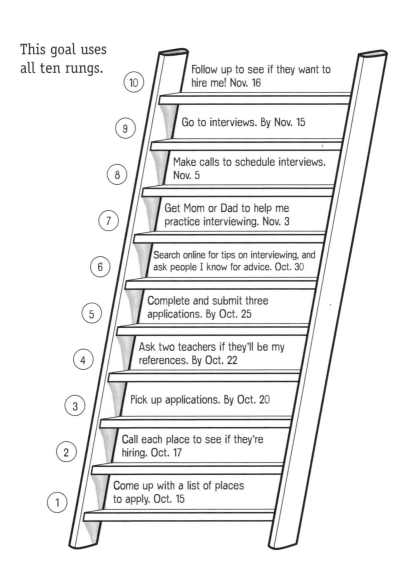

10. Follow up to see if they want to hire me! Nov. 16

9. Go to interviews. By Nov. 15

8. Make calls to schedule interviews. Nov. 5

7. Get Mom or Dad to help me practice interviewing. Nov. 3

6. Search online for tips on interviewing, and ask people I know for advice. Oct. 30

5. Complete and submit three applications. By Oct. 25

4. Ask two teachers if they'll be my references. By Oct. 22

3. Pick up applications. By Oct. 20

2. Call each place to see if they're hiring. Oct. 17

1. Come up with a list of places to apply. Oct. 15

SAMPLE GOAL LADDER

Junior Year:

My goal: _Get into a college of my choice._

My deadline: _By mid-May of my senior year._

My signature: _Ahmad S._

This long-term goal needs one Goal Ladder and one Extension Ladder.

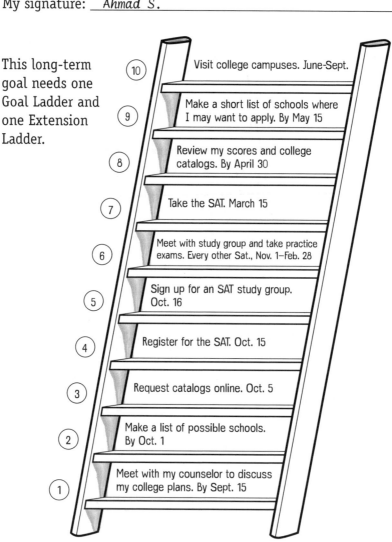

10 — Visit college campuses. June-Sept.

9 — Make a short list of schools where I may want to apply. By May 15

8 — Review my scores and college catalogs. By April 30

7 — Take the SAT. March 15

6 — Meet with study group and take practice exams. Every other Sat., Nov. 1–Feb. 28

5 — Sign up for an SAT study group. Oct. 16

4 — Register for the SAT. Oct. 15

3 — Request catalogs online. Oct. 5

2 — Make a list of possible schools. By Oct. 1

1 — Meet with my counselor to discuss my college plans. By Sept. 15

SAMPLE EXTENSION LADDER

Senior Year:

My goal: Get into a college of my choice.

My deadline: By mid-May of my senior year.

My signature: *Ahmad S.*

This is the
Extension Ladder
for Ahmad's goal!

20 — Send deposit to college of my choice! By May 15

19 — Make my decision. During first week of May

18 — Apply for scholarships. By March 31

17 — Arrange and complete interviews. By Feb. 15

16 — Apply for financial aid. By Jan. 15

15 — Mail completed applications and essays. By Nov. 30.

14 — Investigate college scholarships. By Nov. 15

13 — Complete applications. By Oct. 30

12 — Draft essays and get teacher recommendations. By Oct. 15

11 — Select my top three to five schools. By Sept. 1

Add to your
Goal Tracker!

CONVERSATiON STARTERS: WHAT ARE YOUR GOALS?

Ask these questions of friends, family members, or other people in your life.

What are some of your short-term and long-term goals?

How do you balance the goals that you'll reach in the next month with ones that will take years to achieve?

Do you like to have lots of goals at once, or do you focus on one major goal at a time?

Form #10 continued . . .

What's the biggest goal you've ever reached? What was the key to your success?

How do you decide what steps to take to reach your goals? And how do you keep track of the steps?

What advice do you have about setting goals and reaching them?

PART 4

STAY ON
TRACK

10 STRATEGIES FOR SUCCESS

> "The best way to predict the future is to invent it."
> —Alan Kay, computer scientist

Congratulations! You've dreamed your dreams, set a goal, and developed your Goal Ladder. Even if you haven't reached the first rung yet, you've taken at least one action to move yourself closer to it. That's good, but the fact is that one step isn't going to get you where you want to go. Instead, you need to figure out how to make progress, day in and day out. That's exactly what Part 4 is all about: staying on track so you can make steady rung-by-rung progress toward your goal. You'll learn ten strategies for moving forward. They are:

Strategy #1: Manage your time.
Strategy #2: Boost your confidence.
Strategy #3: Power up the positive.
Strategy #4: Visualize your success.
Strategy #5: Ask for help.
Strategy #6: Surround yourself with supporters.
Strategy #7: Use role models to guide and inspire you.
Strategy #8: Motivate yourself with rewards.
Strategy #9: Measure what you treasure.
Strategy #10: Inspire yourself with words.

STRATEGY #1: MANAGE YOUR TIME

> "This is the key to time management: to see the value of every moment." —Menachem Mendel Schneerson, rabbi

There are 1,440 minutes in every day. How are you using yours? If you're like many people, you may be spending a lot of your waking minutes in ways that have nothing to do with your goals. If you've been telling yourself, "I don't have time for this," "I'll do it later," or "I'll start tomorrow," you might be procrastinating.

If you're procrastinating, you have plenty of company. Everyone does it at one time or another. But if you find yourself never having any time, making endless excuses, or delaying for so long that your goal is becoming a distant memory (and making you feel guilty), ask yourself why. Are you . . .

Hot Tip

If you feel like you don't have time for your goals, try tracking how you spend your time. Record what you're doing in ten-minute increments. Include important things such as studying, attending practice, or eating meals. Also include time spent texting friends, using social media, complaining about things you don't like, or playing games on a phone or computer. Sometimes these activities turn us into zombies . . . and before we know it, the five-minute break we meant to take has turned into several hours. If your tracking reveals a pattern you aren't happy with, make a focused effort to change it.

- ✔ convinced you won't be able do a good job?

- ✔ unsure what to do first?

- ✔ worried about disappointing someone?

- ✔ waiting for the "perfect" time to produce "perfect" results?

Whatever your answers, knowing a bit more about procrastination and how to overcome it can help. When you're faced with doing something you'd rather not do—even if it's something you know you'll be glad to have done—you stimulate an area of your brain associated with pain. And your brain, naturally enough, looks for a way to stop the pain by switching your attention to something else, typically something more pleasant.

But here's what you need to know: science has proven that once you start the unpleasant task you've been avoiding— your history report, your science homework, or your laundry—your pain will soon disappear.

Fourteen-year-old Zack has learned that firsthand: "Sometimes it's really hard to stop sitting around and doing nothing, but once I start doing something, like homework or playing my guitar, I usually keep going. The hard part is getting started."

Zack's right: getting started is hard. But it's also necessary! One simple but highly effective tool can help: a **timer**. You can use the timer on your phone or borrow one from your kitchen. Set it for twenty-five minutes (even fifteen will do), and then focus your attention on the task at hand. Don't answer the phone, look for your missing shoe, or ask your sister what music she's listening to. Instead, stay focused on what you're doing.

Then, when the timer goes off, reward yourself with a small treat—your favorite song, a few minutes on social media, five minutes of texting with your friends. This sort of intense mental workout followed by a brief period of relaxation is great for getting things done.

GOAL GETTERS iN ACTioN

Time's Up: Move On

Fifteen-year-old **Clare** uses her phone's timer to stay on task. For example, for her current events class, she gives herself ten minutes to find an event and read about it. When the timer goes off, she stops reading and starts writing. "Otherwise, I'd be surfing the Web all day but never get my assignment done," says Clare.

Madeline, age eighteen, also uses her phone's timer to help her keep focused. "If I'm doing homework or studying for a test, I work for an hour and then take a ten-minute break. But I set my timer to make sure I get back to work when my ten minutes are up."

Two More Tools that Rule

In addition to a timer, two other important tools can help you keep climbing toward your goals: a calendar and a to-do list.

A weekly or monthly **calendar** helps you see your days, weeks, and months at a glance. You can use it (or a daily planner) to keep track of upcoming tests, homework assignments, appointments, birthdays, and other scheduled activities—and, of course, your Goal Ladder deadlines. Once you start using a calendar or daily planner, you'll find (as many other Goal Getters have) that keeping tabs on what you have going on—in writing—encourages you to plan your time better.

A **to-do list** is another helpful time management tool. You can create these lists for each day or each week, depending on what works best for you. You may want to organize lists into categories like school, goals, home, and so on, or you may prefer one big list that includes everything. Start by listing your tasks. Then put them in order of importance, with your goals and other high-priority items at the top of the list. As you complete each task, cross it off. After you've crossed off several items, make a new list of the things you still have to do. That way, you'll be better able to focus on what's left.

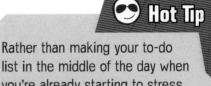

Hot Tip

Rather than making your to-do list in the middle of the day when you're already starting to stress about getting everything done, create it the night before. Research shows that making your list ahead of time engages your subconscious mind, which will start working out ways to accomplish your to-dos while you're tidying your room, taking a shower, and even sleeping. Having such a list also frees up valuable space in your brain—space you can use to solve a problem or memorize a poem.

"My daily schedule as a homeschooler can be quite fluid. To keep myself on track, I usually make a rough week-by-week plan, and then adjust it to account for the unexpected." —Isaac, 18

"Before I go to sleep, I write my to-dos on a piece of paper and tape it to my bedroom door. Then when I wake up I see what I need to get done." —Wai Wai, 13

"For schoolwork, I use a paper planner. I like being neat and organized, so I write everything out and put little checkboxes next to each item. Then, as I complete items, I check them off. I sometimes use different colored pens and color code my to-dos. Items due on Mondays are red, those due on Tuesdays are orange, and so forth. That way, I can look at my planner and ask, 'What are all the red things I have to do today?' Then, I make a list of everything in the order I plan to do it." —Amy, 13

"I use Google Calendar. It allows me to have multiple categories all synced into one place. I have one category for appointments, one for classes, and one for sports. I can access them from my phone and from my computer." —Abby, 17

Tip the Odds of Success in Your Favor with These Time-Management Tips

In addition to using a timer, calendar, and to-do list, here are five tried-and-true tips that can help transform you from a get-to-it-later teen into a real Goal Getter:

1. **Get in touch with your goal.** Remind yourself of your goal, the reasons you set it in the first place, and how great you'll feel when you reach your goal—or even when you climb to the next rung on your Goal Ladder.

"If I don't think about my goals, I'm usually sitting in a chair, looking at the TV. If I do think about them, I might be doing something to make them happen." —Zack, 14

2. **Use the time you have.** Don't wait until you have an entire day or evening to begin working toward your goal. Get started, even if you only have a few minutes between classes or before drivers' ed. In that little amount of time, you can accomplish something—and even small accomplishments can be big motivators.

"I've done assignments and taken tests in the car, and once I even got my boating license on a long ride to an out-of-state soccer tournament." —Mikayla, 16

3. **Make time.** How much time do you spend (or waste) watching TV, playing games, reading posts online, or mindlessly staring into space? A couple of hours a week? Several hours a day? If you can *find* time for these activities, you can *make* time for your goals.

"My video game playing was getting in the way of my homework, so I gave the controller to my mom. She keeps it during the week, and I get it on the weekends." —Carson, 15

4. **Recruit a "get-up-and-goal" coach.** Ask a friend, classmate, teacher, parent, or someone else you trust to help you get moving. Maybe that person can offer you general advice or suggest specific things you can do to get going toward your goal.

"My mom and I work out together. She definitely motivates me to get to the gym." —Sky Li, 14

5. **Say no.** If you're struggling to keep up with all the demands on your time, it may be time to start saying no to activities that are getting in the way of your goals. Your friends will understand if you can't go to a movie tonight because you have a test tomorrow. They might

even benefit if you offer a compromise such as, "Let's get together tonight to study, and go to a movie this weekend."

"I used to play soccer and swim, but it got too chaotic. Now I just swim." —Kelsey, 13

STRATEGY #2: BOOST YOUR CONFIDENCE AND YOUR ENERGY

"When you have confidence, you can have a lot of fun. And when you have fun, you can do amazing things." —Joe Namath, former American football quarterback

When going for your goals, staying motivated, enthusiastic, and flexible are daily deeds of daring. Some days you won't need an extra boost—you'll wake up feeling powerful enough to do whatever it takes to move toward your goal. But on others, you will need to charge yourself up. What can you do? Jumpstart your confidence and power up your energy!

When your confidence is high, you're better able to make good decisions and take action. When it's not, even the smallest tasks become difficult. You probably already know that the better you feel about yourself, the more successful you are—in school, at home, and out in the world—but sometimes you may get so caught up in what you lack that you forget to appreciate your talents and strengths.

Get a reality check on your strong suits by getting together with three or four friends in a quiet, comfortable place. Give each person in the group a copy of Form #11, "What Others See in Me," on page 115. One by one, tell each person what you like about him or her: the strengths and positive qualities you see, why you enjoy spending time together, what you admire. Be sincere and say only what you really mean.

When it's your turn to listen, listen with open ears—and an open heart. Truly take in what you hear, and write it down on your form. Try not to comment, disagree, or act surprised. Just write. Or, if you prefer, you can pass your forms around the circle, each writing down your comments, rather than sharing them aloud. Keep your finished form—full of the great things others had to say about you—in the Goal Keeper section of your Goal Tracker. Whenever you're feeling less than confident, go back and review all the kind things your friends had to say about you. You'll feel better and may even discover great parts of yourself you've been overlooking or not giving yourself enough credit for.

Learning to recognize your own strengths and good qualities is important. Use the Think It & Ink It section of your Goal Tracker to write a letter to yourself, praising your positive qualities. Try to include at least ten things that you like about yourself and the reasons why. Then, when you need a pick-me-up, reread the letter as a reminder of how talented and capable you really are. Here are some examples of what goal-getters like about themselves:

"I like that I'm adventurous." —Max, 12

"I like that I'm a dancer and that I have a lot of energy." —Kate, 10

"I like that I'm different." —David, 12

Need some confidence boosters and power pick-me-ups? Try one or all of the following:

✔ **Appreciate what you have.** Use your Goal Tracker to list the big and small things you're thankful for. Review the list whenever you feel down or unsure. By focusing on what you have, rather than on what you don't, you'll fill your days with a sense of appreciation.

✔ **Remember what's good.** Recall some of the best compliments you've ever received and write them down. (And the next time someone says something nice about you, believe it! Smile, and say, "Thanks, I like that about myself, too.") You can also take photos or videos of moments you want to remember.

✔ **Let go of worries.** Instead of letting your mind run in circles, grab your Goal Tracker and write down any thoughts that are bothering you. When you see your worries on paper, they may not seem as troublesome. Plus, writing about them may help you find a solution. If not, talk to someone you trust about what's going on.

✔ **Do something nice for someone else.** Pick up a piece of trash, wash the dishes (without being asked), help a friend solve a problem, or carry in a neighbor's groceries. Acting kindly toward others helps you feel good about yourself, and when you feel good about yourself, you're more likely to take action toward your goals.

✔ **Tune out to tune in.** Distractions can disrupt even the most ambitious Goal Getters. So if you're feeling distracted, it might be time to tune out by turning off your electronic devices, wearing noise-canceling headphones, or moving to a "it's time to get serious" area.

✔ **Get a move on.** A body at rest stays at rest. So does a mind at rest. So if you're resting more than you'd like, get up and move. Right now! Touch your toes, stand up, reach for the sky, dance—just *move*.

Here's how other Goal Getters lift themselves up when they need to:

"When I was little, my dad used to always say, 'Is the glass half empty or half full?' Sometimes, when I'm feeling down, I ask myself that question and try to find the half-full part." —Betsy, 13

"My camera roll has become a photo journal for me. I look back on it, especially when things get hard or stressful, and the photos remind me of what a great life I have." —Hannah, 16

"Once, when I got a really bad grade, I cried. But then I reminded myself that it was just one test, and that it's not going to determine my whole life." —Sky Li, 14

STRATEGY #3: POWER UP THE POSITIVE

"Positive thinking will let you do everything better than negative thinking will." —Zig Ziglar, author and motivational speaker

A big part of boosting your confidence is staying positive. Most people—even those who are positive on the outside and seem to have everything going for them—are sometimes troubled by negative thoughts: *I'm not good enough. I never succeed at anything. What's the point in trying? No matter what, I'll fail.* You might sometimes have thoughts like these yourself.

That voice inside your head is kind of like the anchorperson on the news, providing a running commentary about everything that's going on in your life. Most people aren't aware of how influential these internal conversations can be. Suppose the voice is generally grouchy? When this is the case, that voice is an "inner critic," quickly filling your mind with negative thoughts that drain your energy.

On the other hand, if the voice in your head tends to be positive and upbeat—an "inner cheerleader"—you'll feel a whole lot better about yourself. That's the power of positive thinking!

The next time you catch your inner critic complaining, tell yourself you're not going to listen to what that voice has to say. Think of this process as tuning out your negative thoughts and tuning in to positive ones.

Here's how it works:

Tune out:	Tune in:
"I'm so stupid."	"I'm great at ____."
"I'm really bad at this."	"I'll do better next time."
"I really blew it today."	"A mistake isn't the end of the world."
"There's no point to this. I'll just fail."	"I'm going to give it a try."
"I can't do anything right."	"I can't expect myself to be perfect. No one is."
"I'd better do it right or I'll quit."	"I'll give it my best."

If you're having trouble getting started on your goal, open the Think It & Ink It section of your Goal Tracker and list the reasons you aren't pursuing your goal—or can't. Write down all your negative thoughts and your fears, no matter how big or small they are. Now, tear out the list and throw it away. Tell yourself you're not going to let your thoughts and fears get in the way of your goal.

If you want to have a more positive outlook overall, get in the habit of looking at every part of your life and seeing the good rather than the bad. Attitude plays a bigger role than you may imagine in determining your future success—bigger than talent, money, or popularity. When you believe you'll succeed, you put yourself in a problem-solving, goal-setting frame of mind that will carry you through the rough spots and put you on the path to your dreams.

To keep your attitude positive:

✔ **Cheer yourself on.** "Way to go!" or "I can do it!" may be just what you need to hear yourself say to stay motivated and feeling good.

✔ **Let others lift you up.** Other people can give you an amazing boost, even amping up your courage to take healthy risks you might not otherwise feel ready for.

✔ **Let it go.** If you make a mistake (and everyone does), learn what you can and move on. Dwelling on your errors or your failures won't get you anywhere.

"My hockey team just played in a tournament. We didn't play as well as we could have and everyone was really upset. I was upset, too, but then I realized that it was already over and there was nothing I could do about it." —Betsy, 13

"I post something on social media, and the comments I get from others give me a boost." —Zack, 14

"When I feel sad or down, or want to vent, I text my friends and say, 'It's one of those days, let's Skype.' And then we do a joint videoconference. The fact that my friends listen and help me come up with solutions makes me feel really good." —Shauna, 16

Affirm Yourself

Affirmations are another way to focus on the positive. By writing down affirmations and saying them over and over, you can replace your inner critic's self-defeating thoughts with your inner champion's encouraging voice. Here are some examples of positive affirmations:

"I deserve good things."
"I'm really creative."
"I'm strong and physically fit."
"I make a difference."
"I am worthy of success."
"I am good at solving problems."

Hot Tip

Keep track of your efforts to change your attitude. Use the Think It & Ink It section of your Goal Tracker to record any negative thoughts and the positive ones you've replaced them with. When you've successfully converted ten downer thoughts into positive ones, reward yourself with something that's meaningful to you.

Here are a few tips to make your affirmations more powerful:

- ✔ **Stay in the present.** Phrase your affirmations in present tense, not future tense. If you phrase your affirmations in the future, you'll always be waiting for the results. So instead of saying, "I will pursue my goals," say "I am pursuing my goals."

- ✔ **Stay positive.** Affirm what you want, rather than focusing on what you don't want. Say, "I wake up early every morning feeling full of energy," not "I won't oversleep anymore."

- ✔ **Stay specific.** Like goals, affirmations are most effective when they're specific. For instance, "I'm working with people I really like in a job I value" is better than "I've got a job for the summer." Just like goals, the best affirmations are easy to understand and meaningful to you.

THINK IT & INK IT

Using the tips you just read, turn to the Think It & Ink It section of your Goal Tracker and write five affirmations in support of your goals. Revise them if you think they could be stronger. Next, write each affirmation ten times, each time tuning in to the power of the words. Rewrite these affirmations each morning when you first wake up, during the day when you have a few quiet minutes, or every night before bed. Doing so will help plant them in your brain, where they will grow more powerful each and every day.

Write It, Read It, Sing It

You can write your affirmations on index cards or brightly colored paper, putting them where you'll see them often—on your mirror, near your bed, inside your wallet, in your locker, or as a screensaver. Then begin putting your affirmations to work. Read them aloud several times a day until you know them by heart. Say the words as if you really mean them. Think about them and feel their power. Repeat them to yourself while stretching, playing rugby, or setting the table. The more you repeat them, the more powerful they'll become.

You can also record affirmations on your phone or another device and then listen to them. Or, put them to music. You can sing your affirmations to any song, but a catchy, familiar tune works best. Start with a song you know, and make up new words that tell the story of who you want to be. Then sing it, moving your body as you do. Sing it while you're showering, biking, or doing chores. The more you sing your song—and the more you move around when you do—the more firmly you'll plant your dream and the more quickly you'll engage your subconscious mind in making it real.

You might feel a bit silly singing—and even saying—your affirmations at first. (I know I did.) But push pass your resistance and you may be surprised (as I was) at how powerful they become.

If you need help coming up with your own affirmations or want a few extras, see Form #12, "Words To-Go," on page 116. You can print, copy, or scan the page, cut out the affirmations you like best, laminate them, and carry them with you.

STRATEGY #4: VISUALIZE YOUR SUCCESS

"Visualize this thing that you want, see it, feel it, believe in it. Make your mental blueprint, and begin to build." —Robert Collier, author

Visualization is another important goal-getting tool. There's nothing complicated about it, yet it enhances your concentration and harnesses the power of your imagination. What's more, you already know how to visualize. You do it every time you daydream: seeing yourself ace a test, winning an Academy

Award, starting your own business, or helping someone else start theirs.

Visualization allows you to use your own mind to help create your future. It's like having your very own movie and knowing that the entire storyline—including the amazing ending—is in your hands.

If you're an athlete, you may already practice visualization. Even if you don't, you've probably heard or read about amateur, professional, or Olympic athletes who imagine flawlessly executing their moves, calmly and without fear. Basketball players practice their foul shots while lying in bed, skiers boldly slalom down mountainsides while walking around the block, and golfers play entire rounds in their minds while eating breakfast.

Think about your goal. Is there a particular moment that sums up everything you want to achieve? Visualize the scene as if it were happening in a movie, imagining new details every time you replay the movie in your mind. Think about the sights, sounds, smells, feelings, and anything else that can help make the movie of your success feel more real.

Your mind tends to produce what it dwells on. A runner who focuses on not jumping the starting gun might do just that. Instead, visualize the *positive*. Feel yourself holding your breath in anticipation of the word "set" and hear yourself exhaling as the starting gun fires. See yourself exploding out of the blocks, running powerfully stride after stride down the track, moving into the lead, propelling yourself across the finish line, raising your arms in victory, and high-fiving your teammates.

The more often you visualize your success and the more details you envision, the more motivated you'll feel. Visualize when you first wake up. Visualize as you eat lunch, walk to your locker, clean your room, and chill with your friends. Visualize as you fall asleep. Picture yourself doing well—in class, on the field, at work, or while raising money for a cause you believe in. Let yourself feel, hear, and see your success.

Not sure how to get started visualizing? Here's how in three easy steps:

1. **Get comfortable.** Turn down the lights and turn off your music. Sit or lie down in a quiet place where you won't be disturbed. Relax. Take three deep breaths, feeling your abdomen expand more each time. With each inhale, say *I am*. With each exhale, say *relaxed*. As you exhale, let your muscles go limp. Beginning with your toes and moving up to your scalp, feel your muscles relax one by one . . . a little more relaxed with each breath.

 I am . . . relaxed. I am . . . relaxed. I am . . . relaxed.

   Let self-doubt and negative thoughts float away. With each exhale, feel them leave your body. Watch them get smaller and smaller. See them disappear.

2. **Rev up your imagination.** Picture your goal as clearly as you can. Set this image firmly in your mind. Now imagine yourself reaching your goal. If it's an event, picture yourself there. Where are you? Who's with you? If it's an object, feel it in your hands and show it to your friends. If it's a task, envision yourself performing it effortlessly.

   Keep adding details until you can see, hear, smell, taste, and touch your goal as if it were actually happening. Be sure to involve your emotions: smiles, laughter, and even a few tears of joy can pump up the power of what you see in your mind's eye. Keep your mental movie playing for five minutes, fully enjoying and appreciating all you've accomplished.

3. **Affirm your success.** With your movie still playing in your mind, repeat one of your affirmations, or another affirmation such as, "Here I am, doing exactly what I set out to do," or "I am proud of myself and all I've accomplished."

   Then, when you have absorbed all the details of your mental movie, take a few deep breaths. With each inhale, say *I am*. With each exhale, say *a Goal Getter*. Then, beginning with your scalp and moving down to your toes, breathe deeply, feeling yourself become stronger, more focused, more determined, and more capable of getting what you really want.

 I am . . . a Goal Getter. I am . . . a Goal Getter. I am . . . a Goal Getter.

One word of caution: Visualizing your success can be motivating, but if things don't end up going exactly the way you envision—the way you see the movie in your head—don't dwell on it. Instead, create a new mental movie. And remember, sometimes good things *don't* happen so that even better things *can*.

GOAL GETTERS iN ACTiON

Seeing Is Believing

Twelve-year-old **David** loves to fish and is out on the water most summer days. His goal is to catch a huge fish, so he pictures his name in the state record book.

Zack, age fourteen, is in a band with his buddies: "When we're going out on stage, I picture myself being awesome, and that motivates me to be awesome."

Ten-year-old **Noah** hates being photographed. So he uses visualization to make family photos more enjoyable. He says, "Instead of thinking about the photo, I picture chocolate."

Seventeen-year-old piano player **Delanzo** uses visualization to prepare for recitals. "If I'm working on a piece, even one I won't be performing for a year, I visualize exactly how long it's going to take me to memorize it, how long it's going to take me to work out all the notes, and how long I'm going to have to practice," says Delanzo.

Jenna, age sixteen, visualizes at swim practice. She and her teammates grab stopwatches, take spots in the bleachers, and get comfortable. Then their coach asks them to picture themselves stretching, breathing, climbing onto the starting blocks, and hearing the starter say, "Take your marks." Says Jenna: "When we imagine hearing the starting gun, we start our stopwatches and picture swimming whatever event we're scheduled for." The girls imagine diving into the pool, powerfully performing the exact number of strokes needed to reach the turn, executing perfect turns, and so on. When each girl imagines finishing her race, she turns off her stopwatch. "It's amazing how much you can picture in your head," says Jenna. "What's even more amazing is that most of us turn off our stopwatches within a second or two of the times we expect to achieve."

Visualization helps nineteen-year-old **Taylor** meet the demands of her Air Force Reserve Officer's Training Corps program. "There are lots of things we have to do perfectly, including marching," says Taylor. "We march in different columns, and each column has a different step or a different number of steps. I couldn't get it, so I drew pictures of where my feet needed to go and practiced marching in my head."

STRATEGY #5: ASK FOR HELP

"You are never strong enough that you don't need help." —Cesar Chavez, labor leader and civil rights activist

The help and support of other people is another key to reaching your goals. Friends, family, teachers, guidance counselors, coaches, neighbors, and even people you haven't met yet have skills and encouragement you may need. One of the first ways to get support for your efforts is by sharing your goals with friends and family. Have you talked with them about what you really want? Have you shown them your Goal Ladder? If not, now's the perfect time to share your goal and ask for help.

There are three basic types of help most people need to keep moving toward a goal: get-there help, know-how help, and feel-good help.

Get-there help is the practical stuff you need to climb your Goal Ladder and reach your goal. For example, a ride to and from meetings or practices, money for supplies or lessons, or a chaperone to escort you on an out-of-town trip.

Get-there help often comes from family members, friends, and other people you already know. Depending on what you need, it may also come from your school or a service organization. It can even come from someone you don't know.

Know-how help teaches you what you need to know to reach your goal. Maybe you've heard yourself saying, "I'd like to finish my homework, but I don't know how," or "I'd start on my goal, but I don't know what to do." If so, you're not alone. Nearly everyone has thoughts like these, particularly when starting something new. Instead of turning these thoughts into an excuse to give up, use them to motivate yourself to ask for help.

When you share your goals, you may discover that other people could use your support, too. Ask your friends and others what you can do to help them, and tell them how they can help you. This might be as simple as reminding each other of deadlines or congratulating one another on small achievements.

You probably already do this on a regular basis. Whenever you ask someone to explain a math problem or show you how to play a game, you're getting someone with know-how to teach you what you want to learn. You're doing the same thing when you watch a YouTube video on how to build a motor or perform a new gymnastics move.

You can do the same thing for your goals. What do you need to know to keep climbing your Goal Ladder? Visit the library or go online for answers. Text a friend. Talk to your parents, teachers, or coaches. Or look for helpful classes or camps in your area. Your community center or school guidance counselor can be a resource, too.

Feel-good help is for those inevitable days when, no matter how hard you try, it's almost impossible to feel good about yourself and what you're doing. You may be cruising along, enjoying a great week, only to be suddenly brought up short. You get to school late, argue with your best friend, make a mental error that costs your team a run, forget someone's birthday, and wake up in the middle of the night only to realize that you didn't think about your Goal Ladder once the entire day. That's when you need feel-good help. (And, of course, it doesn't hurt to have it at other times as well.)

A hug from your mom or dad, a compliment from a teacher, or a "Great job!" from a friend are all things that can help you feel good about yourself. Feel-good help can inspire you, energize you, and bring you up on a down day. Feel-good help can come from anywhere: family members who love you unconditionally, caring friends who know how to listen, coaches who motivate you to keep trying even when you think you stink, a stranger who notices your generosity—anyone who lends a helping hand when you're struggling.

Get-there help:	Know-how help:	Feel-good help:
Practical stuff that helps you get where you want to go	Knowledge and skills that help you accomplish what you set out to do	Mental and emotional pick-me-ups that help you feel good about yourself
A friend who picks you up on the way to school	Tips for taking better selfies	High-fives from your teammates
A quiet place to study	Help with math homework	A hot meal on a cold day
A new pair of soccer shoes	Advice on how to solve a problem	A "way to go" from a teacher
A scholarship	Instructions for making something	Pats on the back
Access to equipment	A class on self-defense	Phone calls from your grandparents
A parent or other adult to take you on college visits	Someone with whom you can role-play for a job interview	Compliments from your friends
Directions to a place you've never been	A lesson in how to set up a Twitter account	A text from a friend you haven't heard from in a while
Someone to proofread your college essays and applications	YouTube videos that teach you how to repair your phone	Handwritten notes that remind you of how great you are

Hot Tip

No matter how much (or how little) help someone provides, always say thanks. Thank yous are simple, but important. If you doubt this, take a look at the credits the next time you go to a movie, or note the author's acknowledgments in the next book you read. You'll find that filmmakers, authors, and other successful people are quick to thank others. Follow their lead by expressing your thanks in person, over the phone, or by sending a card or letter. Or get creative: take a picture of yourself wearing the ski goggles your parents gave you for your birthday, or record yourself giving a speech that your friend helped you practice.

Now that you know what types of help exist, it's time to figure out what help you need and who can provide it. On page 117 is Form #13, "Help I Need." Print, copy, or scan it for the Goal Keeper section of your Goal Tracker, and use it as you climb your Goal Ladder. For every rung, ask yourself, "What help do I need to accomplish this?" Write your answer on the form, being as specific as possible. If you need money, *how much* money? If you need a new skill, *which* skill? If you need motivational mojo, *who* can best provide it, and *when* would it mean the most to you? Don't worry about exactly where the help is going to come from just yet. For now, concentrate on creating a complete list of the get-there, know-how, and feel-good help you might need as you climb your Goal Ladder.

GOAL GETTERS iN ACTiON

Goal Getters know all about how important help is—in all its forms. Check out these examples of how other people use get-there help, know-how help, and feel-good help.

Get-there help starts at home for eleven-year-old **Leela**. She says, "My parents pay for gymnastics team practices and my dad and my brother built a balance beam for me so that I can practice at home." "My parents and grandparents drive me to and from swim practice," says thirteen-year-old **Kelsey**. Fourteen-year-old **Manuel** says, "My parents help me with school because they check my grades. Sometimes I think it's annoying, but they are actually helping me. They'll say, 'You should go talk to your teacher about this assignment,' and I'll say, 'Okay' in a sarcastic tone, but I know talking to my teacher really will help my grades."

What about know-how help? Eleven-year-old **Jia**, whose goal is to win a national speed skating championship, learns from her coaches. "They're teaching me how to increase my speed by leaning more on the edges of my blades and doing a better a job of transferring my weight from skate to skate." **David**, age twelve, says, "My dad has taught me a lot about fishing: how to read a lake, where fish are most likely to be, when they're most likely to be biting, and what to do when they aren't." Fourteen-year-old **Sky Li** turns to her teachers. "When I don't understand something, I stay after class to ask questions," she says. Other teens make use of online videos. **Delanzo**, age seventeen, learned to play the guitar by watching YouTube videos, and **Caroline**, age fourteen, taught herself to knit.

Feel-good help also makes a big difference. Fourteen-year-old **Zack** listens to music. "Whenever I hear something really good, I feel inspired," he says. **Abby**, age seventeen, turns to her blog for a pick-me-up: "When I'm having a bad day, I go to my blog and read comments by supporters. When they tell me that I inspire them, I feel more inspired." **Hannah**, age sixteen, says, "My parents have always been fantastic motivators. We talk about expectations and hopes and goals at the dinner table, but they also stress that they just want me to do the best I can." **Elena**, age seventeen, says, "Whenever I see a quote that inspires me, I post it in my room. I read the quotes often to remind myself to keep going, even when things are hard. One that I really like is 'The grass is greener where you water it.'"

Now that you've identified the help you need, consider who can best provide it. Think about the people you
know (people your age, as well as adults), and people you're
acquainted with but don't know well (your friends' parents,
your principal, someone from your faith community). You may
be surprised to find out how many of these people are experts
in one thing or another—and how willing they are to help.

Once you've created a list of would-be helpers, write their
names and contact information in the right column of Form
#13. Whenever possible, write down more than one person,
so you'll have a backup option if your first choice isn't able
to help.

Ready to ask for help? Whether reaching out to a good
friend or someone you barely know, show him or her your Goal
Ladder and explain:

✔ your goal

✔ what type of help you need

✔ when you expect to need it

✔ how much time you think it will take

If you're still hesitating to reach out for help, inspire yourself with these words of wisdom from real-life Goal Getters:

"I've learned that if you just ask, there will be a lot of
people who are very willing to help." —Hannah, 16

"People want to share what they're doing. So, if you
show that you have an interest, people will take an interest in you." —Abby, 17

"You should always know that there are people out there
who want to help you succeed." —Wai Wai, 13

STRATEGY #6: SURROUND YOURSELF WITH SUPPORTERS

"You can do anything as long as you have the passion, the drive, the focus, and the support."
—Sabrina Bryan, singer and actress

Going for goals on your own can be like trying to eat soup with half a spoon. Getting support from others can help you fill up on success. Support can come from the same people who give you get-there, know-how, and feel-good help. It can also come from others who are willing to invest even more time and energy in helping you succeed.

One such person is a Goal Buddy. A Goal Buddy is exactly what it sounds like—a buddy who cares about you and your goals and helps you reach them by holding you accountable. In return, you hold your Goal Buddy accountable for his or her goals.

Ann Bancroft, the explorer who wrote the foreword to this book, has a Goal Buddy. Her name is Liv Arnesen. The two of them teamed up in 2001 to become the first women to ski across Antarctica. They've been Goal Buddies ever since, and Ann couldn't be happier about that. "It's hard to find someone who's willing to help you reach your goals when it means trekking across ice and snow in temperatures that don't climb above zero," says Ann.

GOAL GETTERS iN ACTiON

The Best of Buds

Just like goals, Goal Buddies can come in all forms and can help in different ways. **Emma** and **Amy**, the twins who started Bake Me Home, buddy up all the time. "We've always been there for one another," says Emma. "If one of us is stressed out, the other is usually pretty calm."

Alec, a fifteen-year-old swimmer whose goal is to compete in his state's swim meet, buddies up with his teammates. With the help of their coaches, they set individual and team goals, and visualize their successes. "They push me to be better," says Alec.

Fourteen-year-old **Meredith** enlisted a friend (and an app) to do a squat challenge. They started with 25 squats on day one and worked their way up to 235. "Even when I didn't feel like doing them I did, because I knew my friend would ask me if I had."

Buddy Up

Here are some ways to make the most of buddying up:

- ✔ **Seek a like-minded buddy.** While a Goal Buddy doesn't have to share your exact goals, you should have enough in common that you can relate to what's going on in each other's lives. It also helps if you share similar values and are willing to work equally hard in pursuit of your goals.

- ✔ **Make time for your buddy.** Will you talk once a week? Twice a month? Communicate via video chat or text? Schedule whatever works for both of you, then stick to it. Sometimes just knowing it's almost check-in time can give you the nudge you need to get something done.

- ✔ **Share both the positive and negative.** Discuss your accomplishments, as well as your setbacks. But instead of making each other feel bad, help each other get back on track.

- ✔ **Celebrate success.** Reinforce each other's successes by sending congratulatory cards or e-cards, posting kudos on social media, or giving each other little treats.

Form a Dream Team

Whether or not you have a Goal Buddy, you may want to form your own personal Dream Team. A Dream Team is a small group of trusted people who are as committed to your success as you are. Whenever you need help—whether general advice, answers to specific questions, or instant inspiration—turn to your Dream Team. They're your champions, the ones you can count on to be by your side, even when the going gets tough.

Keep in touch regularly by phone, via text, or in person. Share the progress you're making toward your goals, ask for help and suggestions, and check in when problems come up. Your Dream Team is a first line of defense to help you troubleshoot even the toughest problem or the biggest case of procrastination.

Who might be on your Dream Team? If you've already filled out the "Help I Need" form, you've probably identified a few people you can turn to again and again. If not, brainstorm possible helpers in the Goal Keeper section of your Goal Tracker. Now put stars by the names of three or four who truly believe in you and on whom you can absolutely count.

To recruit your Dream Team members, explain why you'd like their support and ask if they'd be willing to help. Once you have a few members, fill in their contact information on Form #14, "My Dream Team" (page 118), which you can print, copy, or scan for the Goal Keeper section of your Goal Tracker. Keep this information handy so you can get in touch with your Dream Team whenever you need advice, motivation, or other help.

Recruit a Mentor

You may want to ask a member of your Dream Team—or someone else you know (such as a friend of your mom's or dad's) or admire (maybe the owner of a local business or a relative you look up to)—to be your mentor. A mentor is a trusted guide who will meet with you monthly or even weekly to help you grow, learn, mature, and go for your goals. A mentor invests time and skills to help you develop your dreams and reach your goals. A mentor helps by:

- ✔ encouraging you to take healthy risks
- ✔ serving as a sounding board
- ✔ believing in you (even when you don't)
- ✔ introducing you to other people he or she admires and respects
- ✔ helping you address problems
- ✔ sharing different points of view
- ✔ helping you align your actions with your values

Approaching a would-be mentor can seem intimidating, especially if you don't know the person well or if you have placed him or her on a pedestal. It can help to remind yourself that every successful adult was once your age and had dreams and goals like you do. Also keep in mind that most people truly are willing to help others. Some may even be eager to "pay forward" the support they received from others along the way.

If you've never met the person you want as a mentor, start by introducing yourself by phone or email. You can even send a letter, card, or short video. Include the following information:

- ✔ your name and contact information
- ✔ your goal and why you'd like to have a mentor
- ✔ why you think the person you've selected would be a good mentor
- ✔ what specific help you'd like
- ✔ when you'd like to meet and how often
- ✔ a heartfelt thank you

Before you reach out to your would-be mentor, think about what you'd like to say. Just as actors rehearse their lines before a performance, practicing your side of the conversation—on your own or with the help of your Goal

Buddy or someone else you trust—can increase your confidence. As you head into the conversation, be sure to harness the power of positive thinking and keep in mind that asking for help and support gets easier the more you do it. So, even if it seems difficult at first, keep asking. But if the person you're talking to says no, don't take it personally. Instead, ask him or her to suggest someone else who might make a good mentor for you. Say thanks, then keep your momentum going by reaching out to that person right away.

Hot Tip

Many organizations—including Big Brothers Big Sisters of America, the YMCA, and the YWCA—bring young people and mentors together. You'll find listings for these organizations in the Goal-Getter Resources on pages 141–142.

Once you have a Goal Buddy, Dream Team, and/or mentor, you'll want to make the most of those relationships. Here's how:

- ✔ Be willing and eager to learn.

- ✔ Keep a list of specific questions and topics you want to discuss.

- ✔ Take notes in the Goal Keeper section of your Goal Tracker.

- ✔ When you're asked questions, give more than one-word answers. Get into the habit of being open and talkative.

- ✔ Always say thank you and express how much you appreciate the help.

GOAL GETTERS iN ACTiON

The Mentor Center

One of eleven-year-old **Jia's** mentors is short track speed skater Amy Peterson, who competed in five consecutive

Olympics. "I've been to all her summer camps," says Jia. "She pushes you hard, but never stops believing in you."

Sky Li, age fourteen, loves music. Her mentor is Kate MacKenzie, a Grammy-nominated vocalist and close family friend. "Whenever we get together, she helps me with guitar songs I'm stuck on and teaches me shortcuts for understanding chords," says Sky Li.

Carson, age fifteen, wants to be an Eagle Scout. He has two mentors: his nineteen-year-old brother, Callan (who is an Eagle himself), and Steve, a longtime family friend. "Steve takes me fishing and hiking, and gives me advice," says Carson. "He also makes me laugh."

Using Your Support Network

Your supporters can help you think in new ways, solve problems, and bust through barriers. Your supporters can also help you find the courage to take risks and give you some extra get-up-and-goal when you need it most.

That support is just what thirteen-year-old Wai Wai got on the day of his wrestling tournament. "I was a seventh grader going up against an eighth grader, and I thought, 'I can't do this, I just can't,'" says Wai Wai. "But then I looked at my coach and my teammates. They all looked like they had determination inside, so I said a silent prayer and got ready to wrestle. And even though I didn't think I could do it, I did!"

When choosing your supporters, choose wisely. Fourteen-year-old Anna wants to be a YouTuber who inspires others with her motivational videos. "My mom is totally for it, but my grandparents aren't," says Anna. "They think it'll never happen and that my goal is unrealistic. So, I turn to my mom for support." Anna uses this same approach to choose supporters in other areas of her life, too. She says, "When I want to get on the honor roll, I surround myself with smart people because they push me to study more and try harder."

STRATEGY #7: USE ROLE MODELS TO GUIDE AND INSPIRE YOU

> "Role models really matter. It's hard to imagine yourself as something you don't see."
> —Chelsea Clinton, Clinton Foundation board member

Another great strategy for jumpstarting your get-up-and-goal is to learn about people you admire who have done things you want to do. Whether they have started businesses, raised money for causes they care about, starred in their own plays, landed awesome jobs, or just inspired you to be a better person, these people are your role models. Whatever you're interested in doing, you can find great role models by reading or by watching videos or movies about cool people and learning about how they got their starts, where they find their ideas, and what they do to push past roadblocks. Look for interviews with, books by, or biographies of the people who make you sit up and take notice.

Keep in mind that you can also be a role model for others—siblings, friends, classmates, and other people. Says thirteen-year-old Wai Wai, "I know for a fact that in my lifetime someone, somehow, is going to look up to me, and I want to be a good example."

Not everyone is a great role model, or is the right role model for *you*. So how do you pick someone who is? Here are three tips:

✔ Pick a role model who's doing or has already done what you want to do. You can learn from someone else's experience rather than starting from scratch on your own.

✔ Choose someone who has values similar to yours. Take another look at your completed Form #5, "Values That Matter to Me" (pages 38–39). Who has values that match up with your own? Who believes in the things you believe in? Find role models who share your views and inspire your mind and heart.

✔ Watch for someone whose life is in balance—an all-around good role model—rather than someone who excels in one area at the expense of other areas, or someone who has let people down by behaving in ways you don't respect.

As you can see from the examples below, your role models can be people you know, or complete strangers. They can be everyday heroes, or out-of-this world superstars.

"My mom's my role model. She's raised three kids all by herself. And even though my brother has cancer, she's always there for us." —Anna, 14

"Most of my role models are speed skaters. For long track, I admire Shani Davis. If I was skating short track, Olympian Apolo Ohno, definitely." —Jia, 11

"I think Joan of Arc is amazing." —Hannah, 16

"Basketball is my favorite sport, and Kawhi Leonard is my favorite player." —Manuel, 14

"I really admire my sister. She went to school, worked, got into Duke, and still had a social life. She even ran a marathon and motivated me to run one." —Betsy, 13

"My dad inspires me every day with the way he leads our family, the success he's had, and the obstacles he's overcome." —Delanzo, 17

STRATEGY #8: MOTIVATE YOURSELF WITH REWARDS

> "One of the rewards of success is freedom."
> —Sting, musician

Most people think about rewards only for reaching a goal, but successful Goal Getters enjoy rewards along the way, too. In fact, they're one of the best ways to keep yourself moving. They're also one of the most fun parts of goal setting.

There are two main types of rewards: rewards you give yourself, and rewards others give you. You're in control of the rewards you give yourself, and you can be as creative as you like. Here's how some Goal Getters reward themselves:

"I reward myself with chocolate chips: three math problems equal one chocolate chip." —Amy, 13

"I reward myself with my favorite video games."
—Carson, 15

"After practice or going for a run, one of my favorite things is to crawl into bed and watch TV." —Mikayla, 16

"I have a playlist of songs that I play excruciatingly loud and that makes me happy." —Shauna, 16

The rewards others give you can be just as creative as the rewards you give yourself: a friendly smile, a high-five, certificates of completion, ribbons, trophies, badges, your name on the leaderboard of your favorite online game, and even the grades you receive are ways others reward you for a job well done and show how much they appreciate you and what you do. But perhaps the biggest reward of all is knowing that you've made yourself and others proud.

"I decided that I wanted to switch to a performing arts high school for my sophomore year. I'm really proud that I pushed myself to do that, and I'm really proud of how hard I'm working." —Mary, 16

"The thing I'm proudest of is learning Spanish. I think, 'Wow, I learned a different language in a short time.'" —Nick, 17

"When I tell my parents or brother that I have something I'm proud of, like a good grade or a goal in soccer, they're really happy for me and that makes me feel good." —Will, 12

"My parents make sure to tell me that they're proud of me, which is the best reward I could have." —Abby, 17

When setting rewards for yourself, keep in mind:

✔ **The reward should be for a specific accomplishment.** Is the reward for spending three hours on your history report, or for finishing it? For scoring five points, or for not fouling out? For getting out the door on time, or for getting to class on time?

✔ **The size of the reward should be in proportion to the size of the goal.** Mastering a complex biology concept deserves a bigger reward than learning to spell a new word, even if that word is staphylococci.

✔ **The reward should be meaningful to you.** If you don't like chocolate, don't reward yourself with chocolate. Instead, pick something you do like: a bubble bath, your favorite music, a round of golf—whatever will be a personal treat for you.

✔ **The reward should be timely.** If you've promised yourself a bike ride for making it through the chess tournament, change your clothes as soon as you get home, and then grab your bike and get out to enjoy the day. Don't delay . . . or your reward will lose meaning (and its ability to motivate you).

STRATEGY #9: MEASURE WHAT YOU TREASURE

> "If you can't measure it, you can't improve it."
> —Peter Drucker, author and management consultant

When I graduated from college, I set a goal of reading at least a book a week for the rest of my life. And I've done it. How do I know? Because I keep track. I have a list on my computer, and every time I finish a book, I add the date and title to my "Books Read" list. That list now includes more than 2,000 books.

Learning how to track what matters to you can help you achieve your goals. If you want to be a better writer, write more often and keep track of how many words you write. If you want a happier family, give yourself a gold star every day you don't tease your brothers and sisters. If you want to eat healthier meals, keep a food log. If, like fifteen-year-old Clare, you want to wear a different outfit every day for the first two months of school, take a daily selfie and create a look book or a private Pinterest board with your photos.

 **Hot Tip**

When tracking your progress, focus on how far you've come, not how far you have left to go. This is especially important when going for challenging or long-term goals that require a lot of time and effort. Also keep in mind that you may not always be as stuck as you sometimes think or feel. This is why tracking your progress is so important. When you know how you're doing—especially when you're doing well—you'll want to do even better. And if you're not progressing as you'd hoped, you'll be able to do something about it, instead of giving up.

The most effective ways to measure your progress are visual (so you notice them) and creative (so they're fun). They're also ones you update often. When climbing your Goal Ladder, mark it up so you know what you've accomplished: color in the rungs you've climbed, put gold stars by the tasks you've completed, or write "Way to go!" in the margins. Some Goal Getters like to highlight each completed rung in a different color.

GOAL GETTERS iN ACTiON

It's Tracking Time

"I want to practice my flute four hundred minutes every month," says ten-year-old **Kate**. "To keep track, I time how many minutes I play and write the number down on a chart in my school binder. Whenever I open the binder, I can see where I'm at and how much more I need to practice." Kate also uses a journal to keep track of how long she practices for dance, her other favorite activity.

John, age thirteen, tracks his karate progress by displaying the belts he's already earned—white, yellow, gold, orange, green, blue, purple, brown, and red—in his room. His final belt, the prized black belt, will join them soon.

Fifteen-year-old **Clare** uses her phone to track her running. "At the end of the month, I can see how many miles I've run, how my mileage is increasing, and how my times are improving," says Clare.

Mikayla, age sixteen, travels all over the United States playing soccer. "I have a big map in my room, and I put a pin in every state I visit," she says. "This helps me keep track of where I've been, and seeing all the pins helps me realize how special my life really is."

Sixteen-year-old **Jacob** created a spreadsheet to help him save money to buy a car. He used the spreadsheet to track how much he earned and spent, as well as how much he had saved. Seeing his savings grow motivated him to save more than he might have otherwise—and enabled him to buy a car sooner than he expected.

STRATEGY #10: INSPIRE YOURSELF WITH WORDS

> "Good words are worth much, and cost little."
> —George Herbert, poet

When you're reading a book, watching a movie, singing along to your favorite music, or listening to a celebrity interview, pay attention to those lines that make you say "Wow!" Calendars, books of quotations, websites, your favorite social media sites—inspiring words are everywhere once you start looking. Find that special quote that speaks to you and your situation. Then write it in the Goal Keeper section of your Goal Tracker. You can also write it on an index card and carry it with you in your wallet or backpack, tape it to the inside of your locker, or take a photo of it and use it as a screensaver.

"I definitely rely on quotes and song lyrics to inspire me. I even have a little journal where I write my favorites." —Hannah, 16

"One of my favorite quotes is, 'Shoot for the moon. Even if you miss, you'll land among the stars.'" —David, 12

"There's a Paramore song that I listen to that really pushes me on. It's called 'Last Hope.' It's my anthem. I listen to it when I'm feeling bummed out, and it brings me back to my center." —Mary, 16

If you haven't found a perfect quote yet, turn to Form #15, "Quotes To-Go" (page 119). This collection of quotations can give you instant inspiration. You can print, copy, or scan the page, cut out the quotes you like best, decorate them, laminate them, and carry them with you. Or you can put them in your Goal Tracker.

BONUS STRATEGY: STRESS LESS

> "We live as though there aren't enough hours in the day but if we do each thing calmly and carefully we will get it done quicker and with much less stress." —Viggo Mortensen, actor, photographer, and painter

Sometimes going for your goals—and even just living life—can be stressful. Your heart may pound, your face may flush, your hands may feel cold or sweaty. You might get a headache or feel like you have butterflies in your stomach. If any of this sounds familiar, you're not alone. Everyone gets stressed now and again, but that doesn't mean you have to let it get the best of you. After all, your most important goal is to take care of yourself. Here's how some successful Goal Getters keep their stress in check:

"I make a list of what I need to get done and exactly when I'm going to do it. That way, I can see that I'm going to be able to get it all done." —Betsy, 13

"I don't know if it's my body language or if my dog can just sense when I'm stressed. She starts licking me. It's really gross, but it's nice, too. It's also nice to have this warm, furry thing to curl up with when I'm all worked up and feeling anxious." —Jia, 11

"If there are smaller things that I can get done quickly, I do them first. That way, I don't have them hanging over my head. And when I get stressed out toward the end of a goal, I remind myself to give one hundred percent right now, because in an hour or when I wake up tomorrow, it will be all over." —Casey, 19

"Journaling is a great way to relieve stress, especially if there are things you're not comfortable talking about or don't want to share with friends." —Anna, 14

GOAL CHECK

"Before you begin a thing, remind yourself that difficulties and delays quite impossible to foresee are ahead. If you could see them clearly, naturally you could do a great deal to get rid of them, but you can't. You can only see one thing clearly and that is your goal. Form a mental vision of that and cling to it through thick and thin."
—Kathleen Norris, author

How are you doing so far? Checking in is part of the goal-setting process, because along the way to your goal, you're learning a lot about yourself and what you're capable of. You're trying new things, taking risks, and facing challenges. At times, you may feel totally energized. But at other times, you may be overwhelmed, scared, or just plain stuck.

Some people get stuck so early in the process that they never get out of the starting gate. Others find themselves sidelined by an unexpected problem or a hard-to-get-around barrier. Still others get derailed just as they're about to cross the finish line, like the runner who fades away because he or she just can't find that final push. Do any of the following "I'm stuck" warning signs apply to you?

Stuck Sign #1: Procrastination. Are you putting off doing things that could move you closer to your goal? As you learned on page 73, when you have to do something you'd rather *not* do, you activate areas of your brain associated with pain, which is one reason you may be procrastinating.

But that pain will start to go away once you begin the task at hand.

Stuck Sign #2: Distraction. When you finally decide to spend the afternoon working on your goal, do you find yourself doing all sorts of other things instead? Are you texting, cleaning, daydreaming . . . *anything* except working on your goal?

Stuck Sign #3: Lack of momentum. Have you been working toward your goal without making much progress? Does it sometimes feel like you're taking one step forward and two steps back?

Stuck Sign #4: Boredom. When you think about your goal, do you feel *less* energized—maybe even to the point of practically falling asleep?

Stuck Sign #5: Goal? What goal? Has it been weeks since you've thought about your goal, let alone worked toward it?

If any of these warning signs sound familiar, don't panic, despair, or give up. Instead, figure out what stands between you and your get-up-and-goal. A Goal Check (see Form #16 on pages 120–121) may help. Like a post-game recap, a Goal Check helps you determine what's working, what's not, and how you can improve.

Checkpoint #1: Check in with yourself. Think back to when you first completed your Dream Board (pages 27–29) and developed your goal. Try to remember how you felt. Were you excited, proud, happy, determined? What did you imagine yourself doing? Why was doing it important to you? Do you still really want to achieve your goal? Maybe your life has changed since you set the goal. Maybe you've realized that the goal doesn't support your values, that it competes with another more important goal, or that you're just too busy. Whatever the reason, if your goal is no longer right for you, let it go and grab a new one. On the other hand, if you're still committed to your goal, move on to the next checkpoint.

Checkpoint #2: Check in with your goal. If you still want to go for your goal, ask yourself if it's SMART (see pages 44–47): *savvy, measurable, active, reachable,* and *timed.* Determine if you've set your goal too high or too low, made it too vague or too specific. If you expect too much from yourself or aren't clear about what it is you want to accomplish, you might feel discouraged. If you expect too little, you won't care about the end result as much. And if you don't know where to start, guess what? You'll probably never get started.

Checkpoint #3: Check in with your helpers. Look back at "Help I Need" and "My Dream Team" (Forms #13 and #14) in the Goal Keeper section of your Goal Tracker and think about your supporters. Have you asked them for help? If not, what you are waiting for? Call them up, tell them where you're at, and ask them for their advice. Then, get back on your Goal Ladder and start climbing!

Hot Tip

If all else fails, try to get some sleep. While sleep may sometimes feel like a waste of time when you're super busy, it's essential and helps keep your brain refreshed and healthy. That's because sleep clears your brain of toxins. It's like going to bed with one brain and waking up with a new and improved one that is better prepared to learn, pay attention, make decisions, and be creative (all skills important to Goal Getters). And whether you realize it or not, getting enough sleep can make it easier to solve problems, control your emotions, and cope with change. Lack of sleep, on the other hand, may leave you feeling sad or even depressed. So find a blanket, grab a pillow, and . . . zzzzzzzz.

Depending on what you learn from your Goal Check, your goal may need a tune-up, some major adjustments, or a complete overhaul. Sometimes it may take a few tries to produce a Goal Ladder that works for you. No problem! That's why you can print or copy Form #8, "My Goal Ladder" (page 62), as many times as you need to. The important thing is not to give up.

THINK IT & INK IT

Imagine that someone you admire has sent you a note praising you for not giving up. Use the Think It & Ink It section of your Goal Tracker to write yourself a note from that person's point of view.

The results of your "Goal Check" will tell you something about yourself and the goal you set out to achieve.

If you find that:	Try this:
You don't know what to do or just can't seem to get started.	Turn to Form #17, "Conversation Starters: What Motivates You?" on pages 122–123 and schedule time with a couple of adults you feel comfortable talking with and who can help you pursue your goals.
You set your goal to please someone else.	Go back to your Goal Tracker to review all you've written about your values and dreams. Select a new goal that truly reflects your own ambitions and desires.
Your goal is too easy.	Make your goal more challenging by asking more of yourself or by tightening your deadline. This way, you'll stay more inspired and won't ask, "Why bother?"
Your goal is too hard.	Break your big goal into smaller, more manageable goals. Focus on creating goals that are SMART (see pages 44–47).
Your goal is outside your control.	Write a new goal that depends on you—and only you—to complete it.
You're too busy.	Change your deadlines to give yourself more time, or give yourself permission to put your goal off until you're not so busy.
You're feeling stressed out.	Give yourself a break for a few days, while you focus on eating right, exercising, and catching up on your sleep. Then, when you feel calmer, decide whether you're ready to pursue the goal again or set a different one.
You're not getting the help or support you need.	Figure out exactly what you need and who can help. And then reach out!

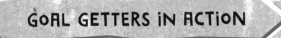

GOAL GETTERS iN ACTiON

Diplomacy Takes Determination

Seventeen-year-old **Nick** was born and raised in Minnesota, but he and his family spent several years in Honduras. Living there cemented his long-term goal of becoming a diplomat in the U.S. Foreign Service, as well as his desire to visit the U.S. Embassy in Honduras. "I wanted to get a tour and meet our ambassador," explains Nick. "I sent a lot of emails to the embassy, but nothing happened. I could have given up, but I just kept emailing. Finally they said yes. It was so worth it. I learned a lot."

Taking the Flight Path

Nineteen-year-old **Taylor** has always pictured herself working for the U.S. federal government. In fact, she wants to be president someday. "I think politicians should have military experience," she says. However, when she applied to the Air Force Academy, she wasn't accepted. "I thought I had a good chance, so I tried again and I still didn't get in. It definitely took a toll on me, but I took it as a sign it wasn't meant for me." So Taylor researched her options and enrolled in the Air Force ROTC. "It took time to get over not getting into the Air Force Academy," says Taylor. "But I love ROTC and all the people I've met there. I know I'll still be able to accomplish great things."

Success: One Stroke at a Time

Hannah, a sixteen-year-old, was in the fast lane to achieving her goal of swimming the 500-meter freestyle (the longest high school event) in less than six minutes—a big milestone. Yet despite Hannah's unrelenting commitment, her times were getting slower rather than faster. Finally, she and her parents turned to their family doctor, who diagnosed Hannah with an iron deficiency. "When I found out, it was kind of a relief because I knew there was nothing wrong with how hard I was trying," says Hannah. "At the same time, I was bummed out

because I couldn't swim the 500 for the rest of the season."
Hannah instead focused her efforts on a different goal: break-
ing one minute in the 100-meter freestyle—and she did it!
She also achieved another goal when she was elected a team
captain.

Going Public About Going Places

"I've always been fascinated by Mars," says seventeen-year-old
Abby. While not everyone shares Abby's passion for the
planet—or her belief that she'll one day travel there—
that hasn't deterred Abby from being vocal about her goal.
She has a website, a Facebook page, and a Twitter account
where she talks about her goal and shares her space-related
knowledge with people around the world. Going public has
brought Abby a lot of support. For example, she started her
website astronautabby.com for a school project about the
International Space Station. For a while, the site just had pictures of her presentation board, but as she got more committed to her goal, other people—including a website developer
willing to volunteer his time—got more committed to helping
her create a better site. Going public has also enabled Abby to
meet astronauts and tour NASA facilities. She was even invited
to Cape Canaveral, Florida, for the first launch of Orion, the
deep-space vehicle she hopes will one day take her to Mars.

Add to your
Goal Tracker!

WHAT OTHERS SEE iN ME

Use the spaces below to keep track of your good qualities and
all the nice things others say about you.

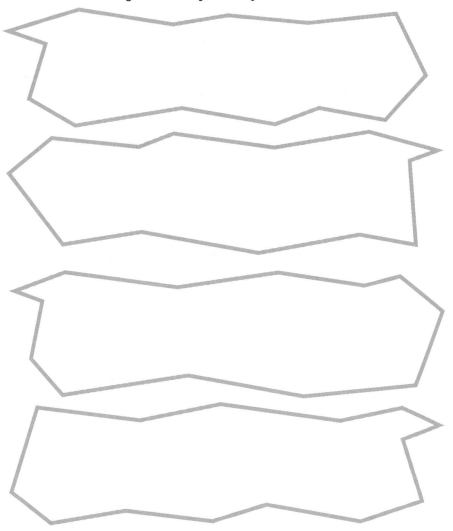

Add to your
Goal Tracker!

WORDS To-Go

I take care of myself, inside and out, every day.

I'm getting stronger every day in every way.

I ask for—and get—help when I need it.

I'm great at setting and reaching SMART goals.

I keep climbing my Goal Ladder, rung by rung.

I trust myself to make positive decisions.

Great things are coming my way.

What I need is within my reach.

Add to your
Goal Tracker!

HELP I NEED

My SMART Goal: _____

What I need help with:	Who can help me:

Form #14   Date: _____

Add to your Goal Tracker!

MY DREAM TEAM

Name: _____

Address: _____

Phone number: _____

Email address: _____

Social media URLs: _____

Name: _____

Address: _____

Phone number: _____

Email address: _____

Social media URLs: _____

Name: _____

Address: _____

Phone number: _____

Email address: _____

Social media URLs: _____

Name: _____

Address: _____

Phone number: _____

Email address: _____

Social media URLs: _____

Add to your
Goal Tracker!

QUOTES TO-GO

"It is impossible to live without failing at something,
unless you live so cautiously that you might as well not have
lived at all—in which case, you fail by default."
—*J.K. Rowling, author*

"Comparison is the thief of joy."
—*Theodore Roosevelt, twenty-sixth U.S. president*

"If you are always trying to be normal,
you will never know how amazing you can be."
—*Maya Angelou, poet and author*

"There are no wrong turns, only unexpected paths."
—*Mark Nepo, philosopher and author*

"Accept and acknowledge your own brilliance. Stop waiting for
others to tell you how great you are! Believe it for yourself."
—*Iyanla Vanzant, author and inspirational speaker*

"Do not wait until the conditions are perfect to begin.
Beginning makes the conditions perfect."
—*Alan Cohen, author*

"Never be limited by other people's limited imaginations."
—*Dr. Mae Jemison, the first African-American female astronaut*

Add to your
Goal Tracker!

GOAL CHECK

My goal is:

Result I want:

Result I have:

Do I still want to work on this goal?

☐ no   ☐ yes

If no:

My new SMART goal is:

If yes:

What do I know now that could help me reach my goal?

➡

Form #16 continued . . .

What can I do to increase my chances of success? *(For instance, find a Goal Buddy or go for this goal at a different time of year.)*

What get-there help do I need, and who can provide it?

What know-how help do I need, and who can provide it?

What feel-good help do I need, and who can provide it?

In pursuing this goal, what have I learned that will help me with my other goals?

Add to your
Goal Tracker!

CONVERSATiON STARTERS:
WHAT MOTiVATES YOU?

Ask these questions of friends, family members, or other people in your life.

Do you procrastinate? What advice do you have for over-coming procrastination?

When things go wrong, how do you stay positive?

What do you do to boost your self-confidence?

When you need help, who do you turn to?

Form #17 continued . . .

Suppose you could talk with a famous person, living or dead, who could help you with your goal. Who would you choose? What would you ask?

Do you have a mentor? If so, how does your mentor help you?

Can you think of anyone who might be a mentor to me, or who could help me reach my goal?

What kinds of adversity have you faced in your life?

What advice do you have for overcoming obstacles?

Have you ever failed at something? How did you handle it?

PART 5

CELEBRATE YOUR SUCCESS

READY, SET . . . CELEBRATE!

> "The more you praise and celebrate your life, the more there is to celebrate." —Oprah Winfrey, media owner and television figure

Have you reached one of your goals? Congratulations! Way to go! You rock! So now that you're a goal-getting superstar, how do you celebrate? It's up to you. As with rewards (which are like mini-celebrations, except they come while you're working on your goal rather than after you've reached it), your celebrations should be:

- ✔ for a specific accomplishment
- ✔ in proportion to the size of your goal
- ✔ meaningful to you
- ✔ timely

What that means is up to you—and those who are helping you celebrate. From dinners out to bouquets of flowers; from time off from household chores to sleepovers with friends; from quiet conversations to lively parties; from dressing up (or down) to new books (or treasured classics); celebrations truly do come in all shapes and sizes.

Here are some ways Goal Getters suggest celebrating goals:

- ✔ Share the news with your friends, family, and supporters. Let them know how proud you are of what you've accomplished, and give them the opportunity to tell you—and show you—how proud they are, as well.

- ✔ Keep a record of your accomplishments in your Goal Tracker. Include the goals you reach, the honors you receive, and the compliments you're given. While you may think that you'll always remember these things, memories fade. Writing things down gives you something to look back on—a way of reminding yourself of all you've achieved.

✔ Write a letter to yourself. Describe the goal you set, why you set it, how you achieved it, and what you're doing to celebrate. Add the letter to your Goal Tracker. You can even record yourself reading it aloud.

✔ Do something nice for someone else, such as throwing an "I did it" party for your friends or baking an "I got my goal" cake for your family. Studies show that being kind to others increases our own happiness.

Take a few minutes to brainstorm celebrations that would be meaningful to you. To get started, think about:

✔ things you love to do

✔ who you like to spend your time with and what you like to do together

✔ things you like to have

✔ hobbies you enjoy

✔ how you like to escape

✔ what makes you feel proud or happy

✔ what gifts you most like to receive

✔ how you'd spend five, ten, or twenty dollars if you had it

✔ what you can do to help others feel good

On page 133 is Form #18, "I've Earned It!" Fill it out and store it in your Goal Tracker as a reminder of fun and meaningful ways to honor your progress and celebrate your success. For more ideas, turn to pages 134–135 for Form #19, "Conversation Starters: How Do You Celebrate?"

THINK IT & INK IT

Take some time to look through both sections of your Goal Tracker, particularly the first several Goal Keeper forms and Think It & Ink It entries. How do you feel now about the hopes and dreams you expressed then? In the Think It & Ink It section of your Goal Tracker, write about where you are today in relation to those hopes and dreams. Are you happy with what you've achieved? If so, brag a little—or a lot. Keep what you write to yourself—or, shout it out for all to hear!

GOAL GETTERS iN ACTiON

Celebrate Social Style

Social media is a great way to celebrate—and share—your accomplishments. When **Shauna**, age sixteen, got her driver's permit, she did just that: "I was really proud of myself. I posted the news on Facebook, and I got a ton of comments saying, 'Great job!'" **Soren,** thirteen, also uses Facebook to share his good fortune: "When I saved enough to get a new quadcopter, I let people know by posting pictures of me flying the copter." Fourteen-year-old **Zack** uses Instagram to share his musical performances, often posting videos of himself and his band. Sixteen-year-old **Mary** also goes online to share the songs she records. Personal blogs are another way to share success. When seventeen-year-old **Abby** was named one of Scholastic's "Eight Coolest Kids" of the year, she posted the news on her blog. **Nick**, also seventeen, uses his blog to share progress toward his goal of becoming a diplomat.

PAY IT FORWARD

You probably appreciate it when people notice your hard work and take time to celebrate your success. What about doing the same for others? You can easily offer your congratulations or say, "That was great!" Here are some more ways to help other people celebrate their success:

✔ When a friend reaches a goal, ask if you can spread the news. If your friend agrees, let others know what he or she accomplished and how proud you are.

✔ Write a letter to your school or local newspaper telling about a friend's achievements.

✔ Send a congratulations card. Cards are easy to buy, make by hand, or create on a computer. Increase the value by adding your own heartfelt message.

✔ Tape a "Way to go!" banner to a friend's locker or your brother's bedroom door.

THE END IS REALLY THE BEGINNING

"The world is round and the place which may seem like the end may also be only the beginning." —Ivy Baker Priest, former U.S. treasurer

"Getting a goal is great, but you have to set another to make yourself better," says twelve-year-old Avery. Seventeen-year-old Nick agrees: "I'm not the kind of person who can accomplish something and sit there and think, 'I accomplished that, now, I can relax.' It's more like, 'Now I have twenty other things I want to accomplish.'" So while Avery and Nick may take a day or two to bask in their glory, they also quickly move on to another goal.

You can do the same thing. Give yourself a round of applause and take some time to enjoy the view from the top of your Goal Ladder. And then start thinking about where to go next. This is also an ideal time to take stock of your life: who you are, what you value, what you're interested in, and what you'd like to achieve in the short term, as well as the long term. This will help you get in touch with your heart's deepest desires. At the same time, you may realize that some goals that used to fit don't feel right any longer. If that's the case, abandon them. While you may be tempted to equate abandoning your goals with failure, resist that urge. You're always growing and changing—and your goals are, too. Here's what some fellow Goal Getters have to say about that:

"When I was ten, I wanted to be a scientist who works with human and animal genes so I could help humans grow wings. Now I want to be a paleontologist or a writer." —Wai Wai, 13

"There was a time when I wanted to be a medical doctor, but then I discovered chemistry." —Isaac, 18

"I've always liked art, and I was thinking about going into graphic design, but now I want to become an elementary school arts education teacher. Specifically, I want to teach visual learners, because that's how I learn." —Jordyn, 17

"As long as I can remember I've wanted to be a teacher, but then one day in gym class a girl slammed her head against the wall. Without even thinking I got down on a knee and helped her, just as others helped me when I hit my head. That's when I realized that helping others through physical therapy might be something I want to do with my life." —Alexus, 13

"For a long time I played basketball, and I really wanted to dunk the ball. I worked hard at it, but it never happened. I knew it was bad for my knees and I wasn't super close to being able to do it, so I gave up that goal." —Delanzo, 17

"When I was really young, my goal was to work at our local sandwich shop. My aunt worked there, and I thought it would be the coolest. I moved on from that goal, but I still have one of my other early-on goals: to become president of the United States." —Taylor, 19

And what if you haven't quite succeeded in reaching a goal that's still important to you? Keep believing in yourself. No matter where you are on your Goal Ladder at this moment, you're still the same wonderful, full-of-potential person you were when you started. Maybe you've climbed a few rungs and are feeling great. *Keep up the good work!* Maybe you've gotten halfway there and are feeling stuck. *Keep going!* Maybe you're doubting your ability to move forward. *Don't give up!* Maybe you've run into an unexpected problem. *Keep searching for ways to troubleshoot!* You truly do have the power to reach your goals.

Remember that what others think of you is less important than what *you* think of you. Even if you're a little disappointed now, don't be too hard on yourself. And don't give up on your dreams.

Keep Believing

Even when you try your hardest, life has a way of throwing curve balls. And while not reaching a goal can hurt, it's not the end of the world. Unexpected circumstances, stress, and your own emotions can undermine your feelings of control. With lots going on in your life, it's easy to feel anxious and overwhelmed.

That's why Goal Ladders focus on one *rung* at a time—and why life is lived one *day* at a time. There's only so much you (or anyone) can do. Sure, things happen that you don't expect and can't control. But there's one thing you always have control over: your reaction. You can make a conscious choice not to let unforeseen circumstances or adversity get the best of you.

Yes, you'll feel disappointed and maybe upset, especially if you've put lots of time and energy into your goal. You may catch yourself repeatedly saying, "If only . . ." and imagining a better outcome than the one you experienced. But dwelling on "if onlys" won't get you very far.

Remember, everyone fails or makes mistakes at some point. It's part of being human. In fact, the only sure way to never experience failure is by doing nothing. The player who sits out every game doesn't have to worry about missing a shot—*or* making the winning shot. The singer who never performs in front of a crowd never has to worry about missing a note—*or* getting applause. But is that what you really want—to hide from life and avoid any risks? To get life's rewards, you've got to be part of the action. And that means trying, sometimes failing, but always getting up again—and again.

So celebrate what you've already accomplished. And then give yourself what you deserve: another chance to move forward, either by recommitting to your goal or by finding a new one.

After all, life is a continuous process of identifying your dreams, setting goals, and then taking action every day to get where you want to go. There's never any moment of being "finished," because we're always growing and changing, dreaming new dreams, and setting new goals. Feeling revved up and totally focused one day, and then stuck or sidetracked the next, are the normal ups and downs of the goal-setting process. When you look back a month, six months, or a year from now, you'll see just how far you've come. You're unstoppable as long as you keep taking the next step. Allow yourself to imagine how you'll feel when you have what you really want and are living the life of your dreams. Why wait one more day to begin?

"The most effective way to do it, is to do it."
—Amelia Earhart, aviation pioneer

Form #18 Date: _____

Add to your
Goal Tracker!

I'VE EARNED IT!

When I do this:	I'll celebrate by:

Add to your
Goal Tracker!

CONVERSATiON STARTERS: HOW DO YOU CELEBRATE?

Ask these questions of friends, family members, or other people in your life.

When you set and achieve a goal, what do you do to celebrate?

When people you know meet their goals, how do you recognize their achievements?

If you ever feel like giving up on your goals, what do you do?

Form #19 continued . . .

What's the most meaningful reward you've ever received? What was it for? How did you feel when you got it?

Based on what you know about me, what kinds of rewards and celebrations do you think might be meaningful to me?

If I achieve my goal, would you be willing to help me celebrate my success? If so, how?

The next time you achieve a goal, what can I do to help you celebrate your success?

GOAL-GETTER RESOURCES

BOOKS

(Nonfiction)

The Art of Self-Directed Learning: 23 Tips for Giving Yourself an Unconventional Education by Blake Boles (South Lake Tahoe, CA: Tells Peak Press, 2014). A collection of twenty-three stories and insights gathered during a decade of research, interviews, and adventures, this book may inspire you to go beyond the four walls of traditional learning to develop your own "one-size-doesn't-fit-all" education.

Be a Changemaker: How to Start Something That Matters by Laurie Anne Thompson (New York: Simon Pulse/Beyond Words, 2014). If you're looking for a roadmap for creating real change in your school or community, this book can help. You'll learn how to get in touch with your passions and how to use digital tools and the principles of social entrepreneurship to make a meaningful difference.

Change the Way You See Everything Through Asset-Based Thinking for Teens by Kathryn D. Cramer, Ph.D., and Hank Wasiak (Philadelphia: Running Press Kids, 2009). This book introduces asset-based thinking and how it can help you set and achieve goals. Highly interactive, fun, and engaging, the book links to a website where you can upload information, collaborate, and share your goals with others.

Creative Visualization: Use the Power of Your Imagination to Create What You Want in Your Life by Shakti Gawain (Novato, CA: New World Library, 2002). This guide teaches you how to use the power of your imagination to change habits, improve self-esteem, and achieve goals.

Fighting Invisible Tigers: Stress Management for Teens by Earl Hipp (Minneapolis: Free Spirit Publishing, 2008). This book offers proven techniques for dealing with stressful situations in school, at home, and among friends. Learn how stress affects health and decision making, and how to manage stress in positive ways.

The Happiness of Pursuit: Finding the Quest that Will Bring Purpose to Your Life by Chris Guillebeau (New York: Harmony Press, 2014). Chris Guillebeau set a goal of visiting every country in the world by the age of thirty-five. Along the way, he discovered all sorts of people pursuing their own challenging and life-changing quests.

I Am Malala: The Girl Who Stood Up for Education and Was Shot by the Taliban by Malala Yousafzai and Christina Lamb (New York: Little, Brown and Company, 2013). This inspirational memoir tells the story of Malala Yousafzai's fight for women's education in her home country of Pakistan and beyond. Since surviving being shot by the Taliban, Malala has become a global symbol of peaceful protest and the youngest recipient ever of the Nobel Peace Prize.

The Innovators: How a Group of Hackers, Geniuses, and Geeks Created the Digital Revolution by Walter Isaacson (New York: Simon & Schuster, 2014). This book profiles individuals involved in the modern digital revolution. Focusing on the creativity, innovation, and collaboration involved in creating the devices we depend on today, this book demonstrates the power of goals and how they can be transformed from intangible to tangible.

In Their Shoes: Extraordinary Women Describe Their Amazing Careers by Deborah Reber (New York: Simon Pulse, 2015). Have you ever wondered what an average day looks like for a forensic scientist or a journalist? This book takes you behind-the-scenes and into the lives of fifty women who excel in their professions.

Make the Grade: Everything You Need to Study Better, Stress Less, and Succeed in School by Lesley Schwartz Martin (San Francisco: Zest Books, 2013). This book breaks down a typical school week and offers multiple tips for how to study, save time, boost confidence, balance academic responsibilities with extracurricular activities, and ultimately succeed in school.

Mountains Beyond Mountains (Adapted for Young People): The Quest of Dr. Paul Farmer, A Man Who Would Cure the World by Tracy Kidder and Michael French (New York: Ember, 2014). This book follows Dr. Paul Farmer and his quest to improve health policy around the world, especially for people living in poverty. From Peru to Russia, from Siberia to Haiti (the location that inspired his life work), the authors document the steps Farmer takes on a daily basis to put his humanitarian goals into action.

No Horizon Is So Far: Two Women and Their Historic Journey Across Antarctica by Liv Arnesen, Ann Bancroft, and Cheryl Dahle (New York: Penguin Books, 2004). This book tells the incredible journey of Liv Arnesen and Ann Bancroft (author of this book's foreword) as they strive to become the first women to cross Antarctica. But the book is about more than just their own personal goals. They also wrote it to inspire young people around the world to go after their dreams. This is a truly inspirational book on the power of perseverance, strength, and optimism.

No Summit Out of Sight: The True Story of the Youngest Person to Climb the Seven Summits by Jordan Romero and Linda LeBlanc (New York: Simon and Schuster, 2014). Jordan Romero recounts each of the treks he took to become the youngest person in the world to climb the tallest mountain on each continent. Inspired by a goal he set at the age of nine, he details how he built on that goal and six years later, at the age of fifteen, achieved it.

The Person Who Changed My Life: Prominent Americans Recall Their Mentors, edited by Matilda Cuomo (Emmaus, PA: Rodale Books, 2011). With a foreword by Hillary Clinton, this is a collection of essays in which individuals who have distinguished themselves in their fields write about the men and women who served as their mentors. Contributors include Walter Cronkite, Larry King, Elie Wiesel, Marian Wright Edelman, Julia Child, Gloria Estefan, and Dina Merrill.

The 7 Habits of Highly Effective Teens: The Ultimate Teenage Success Guide by Sean Covey (New York: Touchstone, 2014). This book provides a step-by-step guide to help you improve self-esteem, build friendships, resist peer pressure, achieve your goals, get along with others, tackle cyberbullying, navigate social media, and more.

Steal Like an Artist: 10 Things Nobody Told You About Being Creative (New York: Workman Publishing Company, 2012) and *Show Your Work: 10 Ways to Share Your Creativity and Get Discovered* (New York: Workman Publishing Company, 2014), both by Austin Kleon. Most famous for his newspaper-blackout poems, Austin Kleon puts forth a manifesto for the digital age in these quick-read books. His premise is that we are all creative and can make the most of our creativity (and ourselves) by tapping into the creativity of others and sharing our own. The books are a must-read for anyone wanting to succeed as an artist or entrepreneur.

Steve Jobs: The Man Who Thought Different by Karen Blumenthal (New York: Square Fish, 2012). The name Steve Jobs is synonymous with Apple and many products considered staples of the digital revolution—but what inspired him to create these products? From adolescence to adulthood and every Mac iteration in between, this book provides insights into Jobs's personal goals and the technological vision he had for the world.

Turning 15 on the Road to Freedom: My Story of the Selma Voting Rights March by Elspeth Leacock, Susan Buckley, and Lynda Blackmon Lowery (New York: Dial Books, 2015). Lynda Blackmon Lowery was the youngest marcher involved in the 1965 voting rights march from Selma to Montgomery, Alabama. By her fifteenth birthday, she had been jailed eleven times for fighting for her beliefs. In this memoir, she reflects on how her goals and values aligned with the civil rights movement, and how it feels to be a part of American history.

BOOKS

(Fiction)

Not all of these books are about teens reaching their goals, but they have inspired many readers who have gone on to do great things. I hope they also inspire and encourage you as you work toward your own goals.

The Absolutely True Diary of a Part-Time Indian by Sherman Alexie (New York: Little Brown Books for Young Readers, 2009). This witty and moving semiautobiographical novel follows fourteen-year-old Junior, an aspiring cartoonist, as he transfers out of his school on the Spokane Indian Reservation and into a mostly white school in a nearby farming town.

Brown Girl Dreaming by Jacqueline Woodson (New York: Nancy Paulsen Books, 2014). In this inspiring Newbery Honor Book, Jacqueline Woodson uses poetry to share her coming of age story and her experiences with multiculturalism, race, history, and the civil rights movement.

Orphan Train by Christina Baker Kline (New York: William Morrow, 2013). Molly is on the brink of "aging out" of the foster care system. A mandated community service project helping an elderly woman, Vivian, sort through her belongings is the only thing keeping Molly going. What unfolds between the two is an unlikely story of friendship and support as they help each other solve long-held mysteries.

Out of the Dust by Karen Hesse (New York: Great Source, 2009). Written in first-person, free-verse poems, this book depicts the life of Billie Jo and her family as they try to survive the dust bowl years of the Great Depression.

Pay It Forward: A Novel by Catherine Ryan Hyde (New York: Simon & Schuster, 2000). "Think of an idea for world change, and put it into action." That's the school assignment Trevor tries to fulfill by creating a new twist on the pyramid scheme. He decides to do three good deeds stipulating that each of the people he helps do likewise.

Return to Sender by Julia Alvarez (New York: Yearling, 2010). This book follows the intertwining lives of Tyler (a boy who lives on a farm on the brink of foreclosure in Vermont) and Mari (the daughter of the migrant Mexican workers Tyler's father hires to work the farm after he is injured). It is a story of finding common ground and friendship, in spite of apparent differences.

Will Grayson, Will Grayson by John Green and David Levithan (New York: Speak, 2011). When two teens, one gay and one straight, meet by fate and discover they share the same name, their lives become seamlessly intertwined. Told in alternating voices, with each Will being written by one of the authors, this novel culminates in a series of surprising revelations.

ORGANIZATIONS

Ashoka's Youth Venture

(703) 527-8300

youthventure.org

Youth Venture challenges young people to define their goals, create plans for achieving those goals, and demonstrate how their efforts will strengthen themselves and their communities. The organization provides a support network to help young people launch and run their own ventures and bring about positive change to their schools and communities.

Big Brothers Big Sisters of America

(813) 720-8778

bbbs.org

Big Brothers Big Sisters of America provides one-to-one mentoring relationships between adult volunteers and children primarily from single-parent families.

Independent Means Inc.

(805) 965-0475

independentmeans.com

Independent Means helps advance financial independence in people under the age of twenty. It focuses on economic education and on pairing young people with adult entrepreneurs and mentors. The organization's teen camp, Camp $tart-Up, teaches participants how to develop their own business plans.

Mentor: National Mentoring Partnership

(617) 303-4600

mentoring.org

The National Mentoring Partnership works with local organizations to improve and expand mentoring programs throughout the United States. For more information and a listing of organizations in your area, visit the website.

YMCA of the U.S.A.

(800) 872-9622

ymca.net

YMCAs are the largest not-for-profit community service organizations in the United States. They work to meet the health and social service needs of 9 million adults and 13 million young people, and individuals of all faiths, races, abilities, ages, and incomes. Contact the YMCA to learn about mentoring programs.

YWCA of the U.S.A.
(202) 467-0801
ywca.org
The YWCA empowers women and girls by offering a wide range of services and programs (including mentoring) that enrich and transform their lives. Visit the website for more information and to find a YWCA near you.

WEBSITES AND APPS

BrainyQuote
brainyquote.com
BrainyQuote offers inspirational and motivational quotes from writers, artists, world leaders, and historical figures. It also features a quote of the day, as well as a user-friendly search function that makes it easy to find quotes that are meaningful to you.

Elevate
Available from the App Store
Using a series of well-designed, interactive, and fun mini-games, this brain-training app helps sharpen your writing skills, memory, and reading comprehension—skills every Goal Getter needs.

Finish
Available from the App Store
Winner of an Apple Design Award, this designed-by-teens app calls itself "the to-do list for procrastinators." It lets you make lists of tasks and their due dates, and automatically groups and prioritizes them. It also archives completed tasks so you have an easy way to keep track of what you've accomplished.

Google Keep
keep.google.com, or as an app available from Google Play and from the App Store as GoKeep
Quickly capture and save whatever is on your mind in one place with Google Keep. Easily take notes, store photos, or create lists. You can also reorganize your notes and photos at any time as your priorities and goals change.

Khan Academy
khanacademy.org, or as an app available from the App Store
Want to dive into dinosaurs or find out if art history is the right college major for you? From kindergarten to high school and beyond, Khan Academy offers user-friendly courses on just about anything you might want to learn: math, science, economics, art, humanities, computing, test prep, and more!

Mint
mint.com, or as an app available from the App Store, Windows Phone, Amazon, and Google Play
A free personal finance website and app, Mint automatically syncs with your bank account and allows you to track your saving and spending through lists and graphs, and set up personal savings goals. It also offers custom tips along the way.

The Princeton Review
www.princetonreview.com
The Princeton Review is a leading test preparation organization. Its website is a great source of college information, including facts about standardized tests, admissions, internships, and career programs.

TED
ted.com, or as an app available from the App Store, Amazon Apps, and Google Play
TED provides a global platform for sharing ideas. The website and app include thousands of inspirational and informative videos, including many by teens! Check out the "TED under 20" playlist as an introduction to the site.

TeensHealth
kidshealth.org/teen
This site is a great source for advice on setting goals and staying motivated. Search for "goals" to find articles on a variety of topics, including school performance, health and fitness, self-esteem, and more.

Wunderlist
wunderlist.com, or as an app available from the App Store, Amazon Apps, and Google Play
From goals to homework to daily reminders, Wunderlist makes it easy to create a list for anything you want to keep track of. Both the website and app make it simple to sync your lists across devices and to set up reminders so you always know what you need to do.

SELECTED BIBLIOGRAPHY

Abuhamdeh, Sami, and Csikszentmihalyi, Mihaly. "The Importance of Challenge for the Enjoyment of Intrinsically Motivated, Goal-Directed Activities." *Personality and Social Psychology Bulletin*, vol. 38, no. 3 (March 2012), 317–330.

Duhigg, Charles. *The Power of Habit: Why We Do What We Do in Life and Business*. New York: Random House, 2012.

Lewis Jr., Neil A., and Oyserman, Daphna. "When Does the Future Begin? Time Metrics Matter, Connecting Present and Future Selves." *Psychological Science,* vol. 26, no. 4 (June 2015), 816–825.

McGonigal, Kelly. *The Willpower Instinct: How Self-Control Works, Why It Matters, and What You Can Do to Get More of It*. New York: Avery, 2012.

Miller, Caroline Adams, and Frisch, Michael B. *Creating Your Best Life: The Ultimate Life List Guide*. New York: Sterling, 2009.

Oakley, Barbara, and Sejnowski, Terrence. "Learning How to Learn: Powerful Mental Tools to Help You Master Tough Subjects." *Coursera*. www.coursera.org/learn/learning-how-to-learn (accessed December 27, 2015).

Pink, Daniel H. *Drive: The Surprising Truth About What Motivates Us*. New York: Riverhead Books, 2009.

Schippers, Michaéla C., Scheepers, Ad W.A., and Peterson, Jordan B. "A Scalable Goal-Setting Intervention Closes Both the Gender and Ethnic Minority Achievement Gap." *Palgrave Communications*. www.palgrave-journals.com/articles/palcomms201514. June 2015 (accessed December 27, 2015).

Sirois, Fuschia M., and Pychyl, Timothy A. "Procrastination and the Priority of Short-Term Mood Regulation: Consequences for Future Self." *Social and Personality Psychology Compass*, vol. 7, no. 2 (February 2013), 115–127.

Usher, Alexandra, and Kober, Nancy. "Student Motivation: An Overlooked Piece of School Reform." *Center on Education Policy*. www.cep-dc.org/displayDocument.cfm?DocumentID=405. May 22, 2012 (accessed December 27, 2015).

INDEX

Page numbers in **bold** refer to reproducible forms.

ACKNOWLEDGMENTS

I've dreamed of writing this book since I was a little girl. I worked hard on it, but I couldn't have written it without the love, laughter, and support of many people—family, friends, colleagues, and some people I've never even met—who were willing to help me just because I asked. I owe you all my sincerest thanks.

I would especially like to thank all those I interviewed who eagerly shared their hopes and dreams and provided me with so much inspiration. Thanks also to Madeline Schuster for all her help and to everyone at Free Spirit Publishing—including Judy Galbraith, Margie Lisovskis, Alison Behnke, Darsi Dreyer, and Colleen Rollins—for their hard work and relentless efforts to make this book the best it could possibly be. And finally, a supersized thank you to Steve and to all who believe in me. I would be so much less without your love and support.

ABOUT THE AUTHOR

Bev Bachel has helped thousands of get-to-it-later teens (and adults) become real Goal Getters. She set her first goal—sell twenty-five glasses of lemonade—at age five and has since used the power of goal setting to make new friends, buy a car, run a marathon, read a book a week, and buy an island beach house. In addition to writing and speaking about goals, Bev owns her own marketing and communications company and writes freelance articles.

Other Great Resources from Free Spirit

You're Smarter Than You Think
A Kid's Guide to Multiple Intelligences
(Revised & Updated Edition)
by Thomas Armstrong, Ph.D.
For ages 9–14
208 pp.; 2-color; illust.; paperback; 7" x 9"

Bookmarked
Teen Essays on Life and Literature
from Tolkien to Twilight
edited by Ann Camacho
For high school–adult
224 pp.; 2-color; paperback; 6" x 9"

Real Kids, Real Stories, Real Change
Courageous Actions Around the World
by Garth Sundem
For ages 9–13
176 pp.; 2-color; paperback; 5¼" x 7½"

Interested in purchasing multiple quantities and receiving volume disounts?
Contact edsales@freespirit.com or call 1.800.735.7323 and ask for Education Sales.

Many Free Spirit authors are available for speaking engagements, workshops, and keynotes.
Contact speakers@freespirit.com or call 1.800.735.7323.

For pricing information, to place an order, or to request a free catalog, contact:

Free Spirit Publishing Inc.
6325 Sandburg Road • Suite 100 • Golden Valley, MN 55427-3674
toll-free 800.735.7323 • local 612.338.2068 • fax 612.337.5050
help4kids@freespirit.com • www.freespirit.com